Martin Luther's Ninety-Five Theses

Martin Luther's Ninety-Five Theses

With Introduction, Commentary, and Study Guide

Timothy J. Wengert

Fortress Press
Minneapolis

MARTIN LUTHER'S NINETY-FIVE THESES

With Introduction, Commentary, and Study Guide

Cover design: Laurie Ingram

Library of Congress Cataloging-in-Publication Data

Print ISBN: 978-1-4514-8279-9

eBook ISBN: 978-1-5064-0194-2

The paper used in this publication meets the minimum requirements of American National Standard for Information Sciences — Permanence of Paper for Printed Library Materials, ANSI Z329.48-1984.

Manufactured in the U.S.A.

This book was produced using Pressbooks.com, and PDF rendering was done by PrinceXML.

Contents

Abbreviations

Brecht   Martin Brecht, *Martin Luther: His Road to Reformation*, trans. James Schaaf (Philadelphia: Fortress Press, 1985).

LW   *Luther's Works* [Amer. Ed.], 55+ vols. (Philadelphia: Fortress Press & St. Louis, Concordia, 1955-).

MLStA   Martin Luther, *Studienausgabe*, ed. Hans-Ulrich Delius, 6 vols. (Berlin & Leipzig: Evangelische Verlagsanstalt, 1979-1999).

MPL   *Patrologia cursus completus*, series Latina, ed. Jacques-Paul Migne, 217 vols. (Paris, 1815-1875).

NPNF   *A Select Library of the Nicene and Post-Nicene Fathers*, ed. Philip Schaff, series 1 & 2, 28 vols. (Reprint: Grand Rapids: Eerdmans, 1956).

WA   *Luthers Werke: Kritische Gesamtausgabe* [*Schriften*], 73 vols. (Weimar: H. Böhlau, 1883-2009).

WA Br   *Luthers Werke: Kritische Gesamtausgabe: Briefwechsel*, 18 vols. (Weimar: H. Böhlau, 1930-1985).

Preface

At the 500th anniversary of the Reformation in 2017, the *Ninety-Five Theses* and the documents and events that surround them will garner plenty of attention. And yet, over the centuries the *Theses* have become a cipher into which succeeding generations have poured their own meaning, many times without ever having looked at the documents themselves! A display in the top floor of the *Lutherhaus* in Wittenberg, Germany, filled with artifacts from celebrations of Luther and the Reformation, demonstrates our ability to treat the *Ninety-Five Theses* as more of an icon than document, more shibboleth than event. The visitor can see the first depiction of the *Theses* on the door of Wittenberg's Castle Church, from 1617, with Luther writing on the door with a quill, whose feathers are knocking off Leo X's papal tiara in Rome (see p. xiv). A hundred years later, Luther is shown pointing to the *Theses* on the door and talking with passersby. Still later, a youngster is seen on a ladder posting the *Theses* with Luther standing nearby, and by the nineteenth century, the familiar pose of Luther nailing the theses (despite the fact that the sixteenth century hung things on doors with wax) comes to dominate. All depictions, however, contain little or no mention of the *Theses'* contents. As the 500th anniversary arrives, some artists have even taken to painting Luther as an angry young man, scowling over his shoulder, clearly ready to start a revolution against the authorities of church and state.

Despite the best attempts by historians over the past century or so, these images still dominate our imagination and make it nearly impossible to comprehend either the *Theses* or their meaning for Luther and his contemporaries. Based on this research and over against all the legends and stories that surround Luther and the Reformation, this booklet invites twenty-first century readers to consider what Luther said and why a relatively benign action of writing ninety-five theses for debate had such remarkable results. In addition to the *Ninety-Five Theses* readers are invited to consider two more central documents of the very earliest phases of the Reformation: Luther's cover letter to Archbishop Albrecht of Mainz dated 31 October 1517, and the 1518 *Sermon on Indulgences and Grace*. The latter tract, Luther's earliest attempt in German to explain to the non-scholarly world what he was trying to say, turned him into a best-selling author overnight with some twenty-five different printings appearing all over German-speaking lands during the next few years.

These three documents are taken from a larger project, volume one of *The Annotated Luther*, a six-volume collection of many of Luther's most influential works. That first volume (*The Roots of Reform*) contains Luther's important Reformation writings from the *Ninety-Five Theses* of 1517 through the 1520 *Freedom of a Christian*. The volume you are reading is designed for use especially by students, interested laypersons, pastors, and their congregants to prepare for 2017 and beyond. It begins with a thorough introduction to the late-medieval church of Luther's day and its most important practices to help today's readers better understand the specific ecclesial, theological, and educational setting in which the *Ninety-*

Five Theses were written; why the document was sent to Archbishop Albrecht; and why Luther rendered his theses into a far more sermonic form for the laity in the *Sermon on Indulgences and Grace*.

Armed with this background, the reader then is invited first to read Luther's *Ninety-Five Theses*. Extensive notes will help put otherwise cryptic statements into their proper context and identify both the main point and the underlying structure of that text. Here one will discover a world of penitential practices much changed from the ancient church and will find arguments based upon Luther's use of the most recent work on the Greek New Testament and upon his own experience with indulgences.

In the second document, readers will find a humble, pious letter by an Augustinian friar and professor (Martin Luther) to the most powerful church official in all of the Holy Roman Empire of the German Nation (Archbishop Albrecht). Here one discovers that the pastoral concerns echoing throughout the *Ninety-Five Theses* reach a crescendo pitch. The failure of the indulgence preachers to do their job and Albrecht's apparent unwillingness to stop them, coupled with Luther's own sense of call as a *doctor ecclesiae* [teacher of the church], combine to reveal Luther's deep sorrow at church leaders unwilling to proclaim the gospel or to protect the simple believers in their charge.

Finally, the third document, the *Sermon on Indulgences and Grace* written and published in the spring of 1518 and republished twenty-five times or so, gives insight into Luther's remarkable ability to take complicated, scholarly debates and turn them into simple, direct words. This talent will reveal itself over and over again in Luther's career—from *Freedom of a Christian* in 1520 to the *Catechisms* of 1529 and the commentary on the common lectionary of his day, published in 1544. His opponent, the indulgence preacher Johann

Tetzel, answered this tract with a publication that was never reprinted—a sterling testimony to the power of Luther's pen to spark the common folk's imagination. No wonder that Luther was far and away the most published author in all Europe well into the next decade.

To assist the reader, we have appended a series of discussion questions and suggestions for how to study this book. Of course, readers will discover other ways to use this volume as well. The point is always and only to invite readers into a deeper conversation with the past and with the humble beginnings of one of the most important events in Christian history. If in the process they are moved to discover more of the essential Luther, his theology, and the gospel to which he witnessed, then the central goal will have been realized: to uncover the context and content of the original Reformation documents for another generation of Christian believers.

Timothy J. Wengert
Commemoration of St. Joseph, Guardian of Jesus, 2015

Introduction:
Luther's First Reformation Writings

This booklet contains three documents from the very dawn of the Reformation: Martin Luther's *Ninety-Five Theses* examining indulgences, his letter to the archbishop of Mainz, Albrecht, dated 31 October 1517 to which he appended a copy of the *Ninety-Five Theses* (both originally written in Latin, the official language of church and university), and his earliest published German sermon on the subject from early 1518: *A Sermon on Indulgences and Grace*. To understand these three documents is to understand the academic, ecclesiastical and popular origins of what later historians have come to call the Reformation.

Yet these documents may seem to the casual reader confusing: filled with unexpected and incomprehensible arguments and language and written in styles peculiar to the time. No wonder that one recent lay reader of the *Ninety-Five Theses* exclaimed to this editor, "These don't sound very Lutheran at all!" Indeed, without understanding the theological and ecclesiological backdrop out of which all three of these documents arose, they hardly seem capable of having launched such an important movement within Western Christianity, the ramifications of which still are being felt today.

Part of the problem with understanding these documents is not only the great distance—theologically and chronologically speaking—between them and us but also the iconographic place reserved for them in our collective memory: An angry (or desperate) young friar, hammer in hand (or, in early depictions, a quill), nailing (or writing) the *95 Theses* on the Castle Church door in Wittenberg on 31 October 1517. And when, beginning fifty years ago, reputable scholars began to question whether the theses had been posted at all, it seemed to some that the Reformation itself had been called into question. This introduction will help situate these documents within the late-medieval milieu in which Luther grew up and worked and demonstrate why, for a surprising variety of reasons, these three documents really *were* the spark for the firestorm of reform that followed.

Fig. I.1 Luther nailing theses to church door.

What Is an Indulgence?

Most people know that Martin Luther's Ninety-Five Theses objected to the way in which indulgences were understood in his day. But what is an indulgence? To answer that question, one must begin with a short course in late-medieval understanding of the sacrament of Penance, which in Luther's day was central to Christian piety. Indulgences are inextricably bound to that sacrament. In his Sermon on Indulgences and Grace even Luther felt compelled to explain the basics of Penance to the people.

Late-Medieval Christians understood that all people were born with the full effects of Adam and Eve's "original" sin and thus under the judgment of eternal punishment.[1] While there was some debate over the fate of unbaptized children who died before their baptisms, everyone believed that in baptism a person was moved from a state of sin to a state of grace by the infusion of a habit or disposition of love [Latin: *habitus charitatis*]. The grace of this sacrament thereby made a person acceptable before God by removing the two basic consequences of sin: guilt [Latin: *culpa*] and punishment [Latin: *poena*, from which the word *poenitentia*[2] (penance) is derived].

Baptism was, therefore, a very strong sacrament in that it removed both guilt and punishment, but it could not be repeated. For the person who, after baptism, committed a "mortal sin," that is, a serious, intentional sin that "murders" the soul (and thus puts it back in a state of sin and liable to eternal punishment), God provided, according to medieval theology (based upon a line from St. Jerome [c. 347-420]), a "second plank" after the shipwreck of sin, namely the sacrament of Penance, which could once again bring a person from a state

---

1. This synopsis of late-medieval theology is based upon Heiko Augustinus Oberman, *The Harvest of Medieval Theology*, 2d ed. (Durham, North Carolina: Labyrinth, 1983).
2. This word and its German equivalent can be translated into English as penitence, [the sacrament of] Penance, or repentance.

of sin into a state of grace. This sacrament had the advantage of being repeatable, but it was not as powerful as baptism. While it also took away the guilt (*culpa*) of sin, it only reduced the punishment (*poena*) from an eternal punishment to a temporal one. A forgiven Christian in a state of grace could then satisfy this remaining temporal punishment, usually by performing the three good works defined by Christ in the Sermon on the Mount (prayer, fasting, and almsgiving), from which a myriad of other works were derived. These good works helped to mortify the flesh, restraining its evil impulses while giving honor to God and helping the neighbor.

Fig. I.2 Medieval Penance. Courtesy of the Richard C. Kessler Reformation Collection, Pitts Theology Library, Candler School of Theology, Emory University.

The sacrament of Penance consisted of three parts: contrition (sorrow for sin out of love of God), confession (privately to a priest who granted absolution), and satisfaction (of the remaining temporal punishment through works prescribed by a priest depending on the severity of the sins). In the late Middle Ages, theologians debated many aspects of Penance. Some, such as Gabriel Biel (c. 1425-1495), the author of several textbooks that Martin Luther read as a student, argued that a person could be truly contrite and that, at the moment of bringing forth love of God (and neighbor) through such contrition, was then and there infused with the habit of charity and moved into a state of grace. One then went to the priest for confession and absolution not simply to obtain grace but to have him ascertain whether the contrition was real—just as the Levitical priests of the Old Testament determined whether a person was truly free from leprosy or other diseases or infections of the skin [Leviticus 13]. Other theologians insisted that the power of sin was too strong and that therefore, in a state of sin, a person could only be "attrite," that is sorry for sin out of fear of punishment. Hearing the priest's absolution in confession infused a person with a habit of love, changed a person's attrition into contrition and moved him or her from a state of sin to a state of grace.

So, where do indulgences fit into this framework? In the early history of the church, as Luther himself discovered in the process of preparing his *Ninety-Five Theses*, confessors placed on penitents certain responsibilities to make restitution, so to speak, in the community for the consequences of public, heinous sins that had excluded them from the communion of the church. In the western (Latin-speaking) church, each such sinful act was said to involve (at least) seven years of (ecclesiastical) penance. In time, this punishment was demanded not just for public crimes but also for each and every mortal sin of "thought, word and deed." In the beginning, "satisfaction" demanded by the church was not equivalent to the mortification of the flesh that God wrought in the believer, but over time they came to be the same. As private confession became more and more the norm in western Christianity (and was the gateway to grace and to receiving the Lord's Supper), the priest then prescribed prayer, fasting, and almsgiving to satisfy this debt.

At the same time, another teaching of the church came into play. Medieval Christians took very seriously the fact that Jesus had said, "Blessed are the pure in heart, for they shall see God." It was clear that, with few exceptions, Christians who died in a state of grace but with outstanding temporal punishment did not yet possess such purity of heart. To purify such souls, God had in mercy established a place where the last remnants of sin—especially the temporal punishment for sin that remained to be satisfied—could be purged away. This "place of purgation" [Latin: *purgatorium*; English: *purgatory*] was a place after death where the ransomed soul experienced far worse torments than any on earth for purification but where the only exit, so to speak, was heaven itself and the beatific vision of God. With the exception of two saints (whom Luther mentions in the *Ninety-Five Theses*), no one wanted to spend any more time there than they needed.

So, believers in a state of grace satisfied temporal punishment through such mortifications of the flesh as prayer, fasting, and almsgiving. But, what if a person was overwhelmed by such punishment—which could add up to hundreds of thousands of years of punishment on earth and in purgatory? Here, too, there was help from God through the church. In the Middle Ages, it was understood that the church could be "indulgent" with its flock regarding these stiff penalties, lifting them when a person performed certain religious acts, especially acts connected to Mary, the apostles or other saints. (No less a theologian than Thomas Aquinas [1225-1274] had also argued that taking a monastic vow of poverty, chastity, and obedience was like a second baptism and thus eliminated all previous guilt and punishment for actual sins.)

For the most part this "indulgence" was a limited one. By saying a prayer in a particular chapel dedicated to a saint, by giving money to a particular cause, or by going on a pilgrimage to a particular shrine, a person could, because of the church's indulgence, satisfy more of the temporal punishment than otherwise would be the case. This even applied to attending Mass during the celebration of a specific church's dedication. For example, the collection of relics, assembled by Luther's prince, Elector Frederick III, in the early sixteenth century and housed in the Castle Church had a total indulgence associated with their viewing of over 100,000 years!

Then, as a way of encouraging people to participate in the Crusades to "free" Jerusalem and other holy sites from the "infidels" (i.e., adherents of Islam), Pope Urban II (c. 1042-1099) proclaimed in 1095 that those who participated in a crusade for religious reasons would receive "plenary" (full) indulgence, eliminating *all* satisfaction for all sins committed up until that time. In 1300 Pope Boniface VIII (c. 1230-1303) declared a plenary indulgence for all of those who visited Rome and prayed at the tombs of the apostles. This "Jubilee Indulgence" came to be issued every twenty-five years.

It was understood that such plenary indulgences were under the sole purview of the pope as a successor to Peter, under Christ's promise to him in Matt. 16:18-19: "You are Peter, and on this rock I will build my church.... I give you the keys of the kingdom of heaven, and whatever you bind on earth will be bound in heaven, and whatever you loose on earth will be loosed in heaven." The practice of issuing such indulgences was very popular and, in time, became available not only for going on Crusades or pilgrimages themselves but also for contributing money to such causes, including the building of churches associated with the apostles.

Fig. I.3 St. Peter's Cathedral in Saintes.

To some extent, the official theology supporting the granting of these plenary indulgences lagged behind the practice. First in a papal decree proclaiming a jubilee year in 1350 and dated 27 January 1343, Pope Clement VI (1291-1352) attached indulgences to a "treasury of merits" accumulated by Christ and the saints. This reinforced the notion that any reduction in penalty for sin had to be satisfied by an appropriate amount of merit available in this heavenly treasure and released by the one who held the keys, namely, the successor to Peter. In 1476 Pope Sixtus IV (1414-1484), when proclaiming a plenary indulgence to help rebuild the cathedral church of St. Peter in Saintes, France, declared for the first time that plenary indulgences were also valid for souls in purgatory. Thus, one could now purchase an indulgence not only for one's own soul but also for one's dear, departed loved ones already suffering in purgatory. Whether this meant that the pope had direct authority over souls in purgatory or could only beg God on their behalf was still a matter of debate, as one of Luther's theses indicates.

Luther's Early Experience with Indulgences

This was the religious world into which Luther was born in 1483.[3] His father, Hans Ludher (c. 1459-1530),[4] of peasant stock, was a miner and, later, mine owner, but his mother Margarete's (c. 1460-1531) family, Lindemann, included well-to-do citizens of Eisenach (where a relative had been mayor). In part to advance their economic and social standing, the family sent young Martin to school. By 1501 he entered the University of Erfurt and within four years had received both the Bachelor and Master of Arts degrees, which left him poised to enter the law faculty and achieve his parent's dream of having a lawyer in the family. Instead, as Luther later

---

3. There are many fine biographies of Luther's life. The standard, however, is the three-volume work of Martin Brecht. The first volume, *Martin Luther: His Road to Reformation 1483-1521*, trans. James Schaaf (Philadelphia: Fortress, 1985), is the basis of this account.
4. In 1518, Martin changed the spelling of his name to Luther as a theological play on the Greek word, *eleutherius*, which means "the free one."

recounted, a close encounter with lightning from a thunderstorm as he was walking back to the university from his home in 1505 led him to call out to the patron saint of miners, "Help, St. Anne, I will become a monk!" He promptly sold his law books (recently purchased for him by his father), gave the money to the poor, and entered the cloister of the Augustinian Hermits in Erfurt to become a friar in that mendicant (begging) order. By 1507 he was ordained a priest and in subsequent years he continued his education but now in theology, so that in 1512 he received a doctorate, though not at the well-established University of Erfurt but at the fledgling University of Wittenberg (founded only ten years earlier in 1502). As successor there to Johann von Staupitz (c. 1460-1524), who was also the head of the Augustinian Order in Germany and Luther's father confessor, Luther continued his mentor's practice of lecturing on the Bible, holding courses on the Psalms (1513-1515), Romans (1515-1516), Galatians (1516-1517), and Hebrews (1517-1518). Having already earlier been named by von Staupitz as preacher for his Augustinian brothers in Wittenberg, in 1514 he became assistant pastor and preacher at St. Mary's, Wittenberg's city church. He also was administrator for several Augustinian cloisters in the area.

Luther's experience with indulgences was broader than most people imagine. While still a student at Erfurt, Luther probably heard the indulgence preaching of Raimund Peraudi (1435-1505). In 1476 Peraudi was the dean of the cathedral chapter in Saintes and commissioner for the very indulgence that Sixtus IV had proclaimed for his church, a decree that for the first time allowed the faithful to purchase plenary indulgences for the souls of the dead. Peraudi went to Rome in 1480 and quickly became papal commissioner (preacher) for indulgences and papal legate to Germany. Thus, from 1502-1504, Peraudi preached a plenary indulgence throughout Germany, with the money being set aside to support a crusade against the Turks.[5]

Among other places, Peraudi was in Erfurt on 29 October 1502, at which time Luther was a student there. This means that in all likelihood Luther personally experienced the preaching of one of the most popular indulgence preachers in Germany. On 17 January 1503, Peraudi rededicated the Castle Church in Wittenberg as the All Saints' Foundation (where some of its canons also functioned as professors at the University), bringing papal approval to the new university, and he proclaimed an indulgence of 200 days to everyone who attended Mass on the anniversary of that dedication.

Fig. I.4 Wittenberg.

As a friar and preacher in Wittenberg, Luther also dutifully instructed his flock in the benefits of indulgences. An account from 1518 of his meeting with the papal legate Cardinal Cajetan (Tommaso de Vio [1469-1534]) in Augsburg includes this admission. "I once believed that the merits of Christ were actually given me through indulgences, and, proceeding in this foolish notion, I taught and preached to the

5. This information comes from the article, "Raimund(us) Peraudi (Péraud)," in the *Neue Deutsche Biographie* 21 (2003): 117 (accessed on line on 7 August 2014: http://www.deutsche-biographie.de/sfz104237.html) and from Johannes Schneider, *Die kirchliche und politische Wirksamkeit des Legaten Raimund Peraudi (1486-1505) unter Benutzung ungedruckter Quellen* (Halle: Niemeyer, 1882), 117-19.

people that, since indulgences were such valuable things, they should not fail to treasure them, and should not consider them cheap or contemptible."[6] Even though in the lecture hall he was beginning to question the theology behind indulgences, in the early days of his preaching ministry at St. Mary's, Luther did not seem to have had serious questions about them.

By early 1517, however, things had changed. First, it seems that Luther was invited by the Elector to preach at the Castle Church on the vigil of the anniversary of its dedication, that is, on 16 January 1517.[7] As he recounted in 1541, beyond gentle comments questioning indulgences to his flock at St. Mary's: "I had also preached before at the castle in the same way against indulgences and had thus gained the disfavor of Duke Frederick because he was very fond of his religious foundation."[8] Two versions of this very sermon have been preserved. Based upon the appointed gospel for church dedications, the story of Zachaeus (Luke 19:1-10—"I'm going to your house"), Luther first pointed out that celebrating church dedications without dedicating one's heart to God was useless. As if that were not pointed enough, he then began questioning indulgences—at the very celebration of a special 200-day indulgence for that church's dedication. No wonder the Elector Frederick was angry!

There was also a second motivation for Luther to express doubts about indulgences. In late 1515, Pope Leo X (1475-1521) had authorized the preaching of another plenary indulgence in German-speaking lands, this time for the expressed purpose of raising funds to

---

6. Martin Luther, *Proceedings at Augsburg* (1518), trans. Suzanne Hequet, in vol. 1 of *The Annotated Luther* (Minneapolis: Fortress, 2015).
7. See Timothy J. Wengert, "Martin Luther's Preaching an Indulgence in January 1517," *Lutheran Quarterly*, 29 (2015): 62-75. The two versions of the sermon indicate that he preached either on the eve of or the day of that dedication.
8. Martin Luther, *Against Hanswurst* (1541), LW 41: 232.

Fig. I.5 Leo X.

rebuild St. Peter's in Rome. The results of this rebuilding are still to be seen in St. Peter's today. Money raised was also to help Albrecht von Brandenburg, the newly named Archbishop of Mainz (1491-1545), pay off his debt for purchasing his archiepiscopal office and for being given permission to hold more than one bishopric—but Luther knew nothing about these arrangements in 1517. The archbishop had settled on the Dominican Johann Tetzel (1465-1519) as chief commissioner for preaching this indulgence, but the latter ran into difficulty almost immediately. For one thing, the Elector of Saxony, who controlled large portions of both Thuringia and Saxony, forbade sales in his territories so as to prevent a gold drain and to maintain people's interest in his own burgeoning collection of relics in Wittenberg. For another, sales in those places where Tetzel was permitted to preach were slow. In early 1517, Tetzel preached in regions close to Saxon lands but controlled by friendly rulers: in January 1517 in Eisleben, controlled by the counts of Mansfeld (Luther's birthplace seventy miles southwest of Wittenberg); in March in Halle, directly ruled by the archbishop of Mainz himself (fifty miles to the southwest); then in Zerbst in the principality of Anhalt (twenty-five miles due west); and finally on Good Friday (10 April) in Jüterbog, ruled by the bishop of Magdeburg (who was none other than Albrecht of Mainz and only twenty-five miles north).

What did Luther say? This sermon is important because it demonstrates both just how uncertain Luther had become about the traditional arguments surrounding indulgences and what his chief concern was. For example, he wondered where Scripture speaks about private confession and asked "the noble jurists" (experts in church law) for advice in this matter. He seemed to prefer a two-fold division of penance into sign and reality rather than the three-fold division used in scholastic theology. He admitted that the pope's intention in issuing an indulgence was correct and even said that "the trumpeters" [i.e., indulgence preachers like Tetzel] were correct in some respects, and yet "some things are said or understood less correctly."

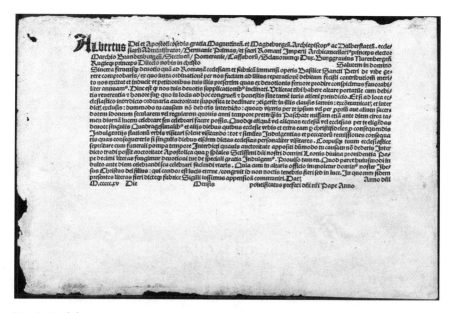

Fig. I.6 Indulgence.

Fig. I.7 Albrecht of Mainz.

Fig. I.8 Johann Tetzel in a Depiction from 1717.

But underneath this terminological uncertainty lurked a theological concern. Luther worried that "frequently indulgences work against grace" (or, in the other version, "against interior penitence"). The people were being misled through "seducers and confabulators and preachers of indulgences and are driven toward security, laziness, and listlessness and to forgetfulness of God and his cross, although our life is still a perpetual battle in which there must never be snoring." What Christians needed "for true interior penance is true contrition, true confession, true satisfaction in the spirit." Through this they are effectively converted to God and trust God in the heart. Such persons do not want to avoid mortification of the flesh but welcome it. And precisely here lay the problem for Luther: "Consequently, indulgences by teaching the contrary (namely, fleeing from punishment and satisfaction) are cutting things short." Indulgences, as Luther understood them in early 1517, were helping people avoid God's own work of imposing the cross upon the sinner to eliminate the evil remnants of sin from the believer's life. He concluded: "You see, therefore, how dangerous a thing the preaching of indulgences is, which teaches a mutilated grace, namely to flee satisfaction and punishment." How can one preach both true contrition and an indulgence at the same time, he asked, "when true contrition desires a rigid exaction of punishment and such an indulgence relaxes it too much?"

So, already early in 1517, while actually preaching an indulgence himself, Luther had deep concerns about the effects of indulgences on believers' lives—not only as they flocked to hear Johann Tetzel some seventy miles away in Eisleben but also as they listened to Luther himself! His worries, furthermore, arose not simply out of theological nitpicking but from deep pastoral concerns. What happens to true sorrow for sin and true satisfaction (good works done for the neighbor), when people can buy their way around these things by purchasing an indulgence? Before Luther had heard any direct reports about Tetzel's preaching or even read the *Summary Instruction* (the guidelines for preaching this indulgence prepared by theologians at the court of Archbishop Albrecht), he was expressing deep, pastoral unease.

Put another way: Luther's earliest concern was not that heaven and the gospel were for sale but rather than escape from judgment and from the law were! His lectures from around this time make clear that Luther viewed the Christian life as always moving from God's judgment against sin (law) to trust in Christ (gospel), that is, from the death (mortification) of the old creature to the birth of the new. Indulgences prevented that very movement by allowing people to buy their way out from under judgment. To use language from a much later era, Luther worried about a kind of "cheap grace" because indulgences allowed people to rely on their own buying power to escape God's judgment. But, since grace is neither cheap nor expensive but free, being "indulgent" was really no grace at all, because such indulgence centered in a person's own ability to buy one's way around the law and its judgment and was based upon the prior good works of others.

This January sermon may reveal some of Luther's early worries, but it is a sermon preached at St. Mary's a little more than a month later, on the appointed gospel for the Feast of St. Matthias (24 February; Matt. 11:25-30) that showed how much more concerned he had become, probably as a result of hearing rumors about Tetzel's preaching.[9] Luther contrasts the "foolishness" of Christ's wisdom with those who "want to attain peace of conscience through their own counsels and accomplishments and their own self-chosen ways . . . ." Those seeking to wash away sins through works dread Christ's cross and practice only a servile righteousness, which "the very profusion of indulgences astonishingly fills up. . . . Through these nothing is accomplished except that the people learn to fear and flee and dread the penalty of sins but not the sins themselves." Instead of embracing the cross, "to indulge means to permit, and indulgence is equivalent to impunity, permission to sin, and license to nullify the cross of

---

9. See LW 51: 26-31, where the sermon is correctly dated but incorrectly labeled as a sermon on St. Matthew's Day (celebrated on 21 September).

Christ." Perhaps useful for the weak in faith, indulgences otherwise "teach us to dread the cross and suffering and the result is that we never become gentle or lowly, and that means that we never receive indulgence nor come to Christ. Oh, the dangers of our time! Oh, you snoring priests! Oh, darkness deeper than Egyptian![10] How secure we are in the midst of the worst of all our evils!"

The Ninety-Five Theses and the Letter to Albrecht

What Luther did next was to study church law (called canon law) with the help of some of the canon lawyers in Wittenberg. To understand why this study was so important, we need to know something about Luther's approach to theology. At the University of Erfurt Luther was trained in scholastic theology and both there and at Wittenberg progressed through the normal degrees for obtaining a doctorate: receiving first a Bachelor of Bible, lecturing on and become a "licentiate" in the *Sentences* of Peter Lombard (c. 1096-1164)—the basic theology textbook since the twelfth century, used and commented upon by every major Western theologian of the Middle Ages—before finally receiving his doctorate. This final degree allowed him to lecture on any topic (like von Staupitz, his predecessor, he lectured on the Bible), to preside over formal disputations necessary for students to receive the next degree and to lead open debates on any topic by posting theses on the church doors in Wittenberg.

But as much as late-medieval theology and von Staupitz influenced Luther, he also was heir to a new movement sweeping Renaissance Europe called humanism. Humanism in Luther's day could better be called "concern for the humanities," that is, it was a movement to recover the most ancient sources (with the cry: *ad fontes!* ["to the

---

10. See Exod. 10:21-29.

sources"]) and to use polished Latin and classical forms of speech and to read good ancient literature (*bonae litterae* ["good letters"]), rather than be content with medieval Latin (which had imported many new words into the ancient Latin of Cicero) or with scholastic disputations and commentaries. By Luther's day, the rediscovery and printing of ancient Greek texts meant learning and using Greek as well. Although humanists (a term derived from Italian universities whose students nicknamed tutors in rhetoric, history, poetics and the like "*humaniste*") represented a wide variety of philosophical and theological points of view, their interest in going back to the oldest and, hence, purest sources changed profoundly how they viewed authority. In many ways, Luther and the University of Wittenberg came to embody this new approach to learning, so that by 1518 their students were encouraged to take courses in the Bible and the ancient church fathers and to learn Greek and Hebrew (for which new professorships were being created).

But this quest to return to the sources also influenced Luther's study of indulgences in canon law during the summer of 1517. Unlike some of his scholastic contemporaries, Luther did not rank authorities so that the more recent had precedence over earlier ones, but rather, like other humanists, he assumed that the very oldest sources were more reliable and authoritative than later ones. His study of indulgences in canon law led him to the conclusion that in the ancient and early-medieval church indulgences and the penalties that they lifted were strictly ecclesiastical ones, having nothing directly to do with punishments for sin meted out by God. This meant for him that later papal decrees, which assumed the pope had authority to lift God's punishment for sin, had misconstrued the nature of indulgences and needed to be revised in light of the clear testimony of canon law, the ancient church fathers, and Scripture.

Already before Luther had embarked on his study of canon law, he had also begun to use the very latest humanist tool for theology: the first printed version of the Greek New Testament. Produced in Basel [now in Switzerland] by Erasmus of Rotterdam ([1466–1536] often called the prince of humanists), the 1516 version published in parallel columns the Greek text and the standard Latin translation (called the Vulgate, translated in the fifth century by Jerome). A companion volume included Erasmus's annotations, where he corrected the Latin text on the basis of the Greek original. (In the second edition of 1519, Erasmus placed his own translation parallel to the Greek text rather than the Vulgate.)

Armed with these annotations, Luther examined what Erasmus said about the key proof text for the sacrament of Penance, Matt. 4:17, which read in the Vulgate: "Then Jesus began to preach and said, 'Do penance; for the kingdom of heaven is coming near.'" The words "do penance" were used as a proof text for going to the sacrament of Penance. But Erasmus noted already in an earlier occurrence of the phrase in Matt. 3:2 that the Greek verb, *metanoiete*, meant something quite different. First, he described how in the early church "penance" was punishment that the church meted out on those who had committed a public sin and been put out of the fellowship. Then he blamed later theologians for taking comments by Augustine about such *public* satisfaction and twisting them to mean contrition or sorrow in the soul. Finally, he argued that *metanoia* actually meant regret after having committed some evil deed. He concluded, "In my judgment, it could be properly translated 'Recover your senses!' or 'Return to a right mind!'"[11]

---

11. Erasmus, *Annotationes in Novum Instrumentum* (Basel: Froben, 1516), 241. He referred back to these comments in a note on Matt. 4:17.

NOVVM IN

strumentũ omne, diligenter ab ERASMO ROTERODAMO
recognitum & emendatum, nõ folum ad græcam ueritatein, ue-
rumetiam ad multorum utriufcæ linguæ codicum, eorumcæ ue-
terum fimul & emendatorum fidem, poftremo ad pro-
batiffimorum autorum citationem, emendationem
& interpretationem, præcipue, Origenis, Chry
foftomi, Cyrilli, Vulgarij, Hieronymi, Cy-
priani, Ambrofij, Hilarij, Augufti-
ni, una cũ Annotationibus, quæ
lectorem doceant, quid qua
ratione mutatum fit.
Quifquis igitur
amas ue-
ram
Theolo-
giam, lege, cogno
fce, ac deinde iudica.
Necæ ftatim offendere, fi
quid mutatum offenderis, fed
expende, num in melius mutatum fit.

APVD INCLYTAM
GERMANIAE BASILAEAM.

CVM PRIVILEGIO
MAXIMILIANI CAESARIS AVGVSTI,
NE QVIS ALIVS IN SACRA ROMA-
NI IMPERII DITIONE, INTRA QVATV
OR ANNOS EXCVDAT, AVT ALIBI
EXCVSVM IMPORTET.

Fig. I.9 *Novum Instrumentum.*

Not only had Erasmus taken away one of the chief proof texts for the sacrament of Penance, but he had also criticized the misuse of the ancient church's practice by later theologians, who turned an ecclesiastical practice of punishment for public sin into contrition and sorrow in the soul. Luther, eager to return to the purest sources, suddenly found support from the Prince of Humanists for a totally new approach to indulgences and penance. His own examination of canon law proved Erasmus's argument. The early church—to say nothing of the New Testament Christians—bore no traces of this late-medieval practice. Armed with this information and driven by his own experience as a preacher and pastor, Luther went to work crafting an appeal to return to earlier and better church practice and theology: the *Ninety-Five Theses*.

The Ninety-Five Theses

By the time Luther began working on these theses, he had also heard more specifics about Tetzel's fiery preaching, and he had read the *Summary Instruction* (the guidebook for preaching this indulgence), which in some aspects crossed the line between an indulgence connected to satisfaction for sin and one that affected contrition and confession as well. Looking back in 1541, Luther rehearsed some of the things Tetzel was reported to have said. Were one to rape the Virgin Mary so that she conceived another child, God would forgive him, "provided he placed the necessary sum in the box." The papal coat-of-arms, always displayed prominently during such preaching, was as powerful as Christ's cross. He [Tetzel] had saved more souls through his indulgence preaching than the Apostle Peter. And, of course, "that if anyone put money in the box for a soul in purgatory, the soul would fly to heaven as soon as the coin clinked on the bottom." Worse yet, sorrow for sin or repentance was not necessary if one bought an indulgence.[12] Luther's memory was fairly accurate, as he had already recounted several of these objectionable statements in the *Ninety-Five Theses* themselves.

As mentioned above, one of the rights a doctor [teacher] of the church possessed was to hold disputations on any subject and to preside over the granting of degrees, for which a candidate had to defend theses written by his teacher. The theses for such debates, according to the University of Wittenberg statutes, were to be posted on the doors of the churches in town. Luther was no stranger to writing and defending such theses. For example, he composed and had printed ninety-seven theses attacking scholastic theology, which his student, Franz Günther, defended on 4 September 1517 in order to receive the first theology degree, the Bachelor of Bible.[13]

The *Ninety-Five Theses*: Posted and Printed?

But now comes a question that scholars have been debating since around 1967 (the 450th anniversary of the *Ninety-Five Theses*): Did Luther post the *Ninety-Five Theses* at all? Given the iconic nature of the event, the original dispute in the 1960s was quite lively. Since then, scholars continue to disagree, with both Lutherans and Roman Catholics lining up on different sides of the issue. Most agree both that the question is not that important historically speaking, but it remains the kind of riddle with which historians love to grapple—and that its iconographic power is unmistakable. The problem arises because until June 1546—a short four months after Luther's death—no one, least of all Luther, had published an account of the events of 1517 that mentioned such a posting. In the preface to the second volume of Luther's Latin works, Philip Melanchthon (Luther's colleague at the University originally hired in 1518 to fill the newly

12. LW 41: 232.
13. LW 31:3-16.

created professorship in Greek), working with his own memory of the events and perhaps notes Luther had made prior to his death, gave an overview of that history, expanding upon Luther's own reminiscences in the 1545 preface to the first volume.[14] Although volume two covered publications from 1520-1525, Melanchthon began with events even prior to 1517 and mentioned, in a rather offhand manner, that Luther posted the *Ninety-Five Theses* on the door of the Castle Church on 31 October. The trouble is, Melanchthon first arrived in Wittenberg in August 1518 and so could not have been an eyewitness to that event. He could, of course, have heard this directly from Luther or perhaps from Melanchthon's close friend and student, Georg Major, who as a fifteen-year-old choir boy at the Castle Church and who could easily have witnessed the event, or from others who were in Wittenberg at the time (Johann Agricola or Nicholas von Amsdorf—the former a student of Luther and the latter his colleague).

Then there is the related question of whether Luther himself had the theses printed, given that no Wittenberg printing has survived. In those days, scholars often simply wrote multiple copies of such documents and sent them to various people (or posted them publicly). The only printing press in Wittenberg in those days, run by Johann Grunenberg, was housed in the basement of the Augustinian friary (along with the kitchen and the toilet), right under Luther's study. Only recently a Wittenberg first printing of the *Ninety-Seven Theses* has been discovered, proving that Luther had theses printed in those days. Melanchthon's reference to the publishing of the theses (which did not necessarily imply printing) was again matter-of-fact.

> While Luther was proceeding with [learning Greek and Hebrew], indulgences were being carried around for sale in this area by the

14. LW 34:323-38.

Dominican Tetzel, that impudent sycophant. Luther, irritated by the man's godless and nefarious sermons and burning with zeal for godliness, published *Propositions on Indulgences*, which are now in the first volume of his collected works, and affixed them publicly on the church next to the Wittenberg castle on the Eve of the Feast of All Saints' [31 October] 1517.[15]

Melanchthon's point was simply that Luther made them public on that day (a day that Luther was already commemorating ten years later as the beginning of the conflict with Rome). Moreover, Melanchthon could well have been thinking in terms of the standard practice of affixing theses and other notices to the doors of Wittenberg's churches, especially the Castle Church, which served as a community bulletin board for just such documents. In a later reminiscence, Melanchthon mentioned that it was at Vespers. Others added that, because the foundation at the Castle Church was the All Saints' Foundation, this was a special time for the "indulgence market." In fact, when the papal legate Peraudi had rededicated the church on 17 January 1503, he established by papal decree that not only the day of dedication but also 1 November were times when attending Mass gained a person 200 days special indulgence. Moreover, this was one of two times in the year when the relics were displayed, to the viewing of which were attached far more indulgences. What later observers connected with the dawning of the Reformation (or even the freedom of the individual!), however, was simply business as usual for a late-medieval professor of theology or, if Luther did not post them, Melanchthon's fair assumption of normal events at the university.

---

15. *Corpus Reformatorum*, ed. Karl Bretschneider and Heinrich Bindseil, 28 vols. (Halle: A. Schwetschke & Sons, 1834–1860) 6:161–62. Melanchthon blamed Tetzel for starting the conflagration.

"Posting" the *Ninety-Five Theses* to
Archbishop Albrecht of Mainz

Luther's theses had a very different character from others that he wrote at the same time, and the invitation to people unable to attend the disputation to answer by letter is unique. Moreover, there is no indication that the disputation was ever held! Thus, it would seem that Luther's intent was not so much holding a run-of-the-mill disputation in Wittenberg but rather to begin a discussion of a church practice that he found particularly disturbing. On all of these historical questions of printing and posting the jury is still out, and reputable scholars have taken opposing views on the matter. But one fact is undeniable. The theses were "posted"—that is, mailed—to one man, Archbishop Albrecht of Mainz. The original letter in Luther's hand with the secretary's notation about when it arrived is in the royal archives in Stockholm, Sweden. (See below, p. 31.)

This "posting" not only indicates Luther's desire to show respect for Albrecht, the highest-ranking prelate in the Holy Roman Empire (and for his immediate superior, the bishop of Brandenburg, to whom he probably also sent a copy). It also reveals how deep his pastoral concern went. His own discomfort over preaching indulgences may be reflected in thesis 39, but far more often did he register complaints both concerning what people were saying about Tetzel's preaching and concerning the archbishop's own *Summary Instruction*, under whose rules Tetzel was supposed to be operating. In some ways, the debate over the posting in Wittenberg obscures what was by far the more important event—that on 31 October 1517 Luther wrote to Archbishop Albrecht in an attempt to get him to rein in Tetzel and to open up a theological and pastoral debate over indulgences.

When the Archbishop suspected novel and, hence, heretical

teaching and turned it over first to his own theological faculty in Mainz for their opinion and then to Rome for its judgment, he started a process that led almost inexorably to the events of 1520, when the pope, in the bull *Exsurge Domini*, gave Luther sixty days to recant or be excommunicated as a heretic and Luther, in response, burned the papal bull and a copy of canon law outside Wittenberg's city gates on 10 December 1520. The results of his appearance before the parliament (or diet) of the Holy Roman Empire, meeting in the Rhineland city of Worms in spring of 1521, led to his being declared an outlaw of the Empire.

The Sermon on Indulgences and Grace

The suspicions about Luther's theology were always twofold. On the one hand, his reduction of indulgences' authority to the lifting of ecclesiastical sanctions flew in the face of hundreds of years of practice and theology. But, on the other, to some readers he seemed to be instructing the pope himself. In the Late Middle Ages, debate was raging over whether a general church council—the assembly of bishops in communion with Rome—or the papacy itself was the church's final authority in theological and practical matters. Dominicans, who championed the theology of Thomas Aquinas (1225-1274), tended to support a papal or curialist (the Latin, *curia*, designated the papal court) position. Others, including the faculty of the University of Paris—the oldest of the medieval universities—argued in favor of a conciliarist position. Because many of Luther's earliest critics were Dominicans or Thomists (students of the Dominican Thomas Aquinas)—Johann Tetzel, the papal court theologian Sylvester Prierias (c. 1456-1527), and the papal legate Cajetan—Luther quickly suspected that their concerns about this second matter had less to do with his theses and far more to do with this curialist/conciliarist debate, concerning which before this time he seems singularly uninterested. And when in 1518 and again in 1520 he appealed to a council over the pope's decision—an act the curialists judged in and of itself to be a sign of heresy—it appeared to these very opponents that Luther's main concern was to attack papal authority. Thus, the third document in this collection is important because it lacks any mention of the papal authority and is Luther's first published discussion of indulgences after the *Ninety-Five Theses*.

But there are also other reasons to study it. In January of 1518, one of Luther's colleagues, the law professor Christoph Scheurl (1481-1542) who spent much of his time in Nuremberg, saw to the printing of the *Ninety-Five Theses* in that imperial city—one of three printings that have come down to us (the other two are from Leipzig and Basel). He inquired of Luther whether he wanted the *Theses* translated into German and sent copies of both the Latin and German for Luther to look at. We do not know if the German version had been printed or was still in manuscript form—no copies of a German translation from 1517 or 1518 have come down to us. What we do know is that Luther responded negatively to Scheurl's request and wrote that he was planning instead to publish a different, simpler German document for the laity.

This simple document represents a crucial step along the path toward the Reformation. First, the *Sermon on Indulgences and Grace* became a best seller, reprinted at least twenty-five times in the next few years. Luther could not have guessed that this little "sermon" (the word could also be translated "essay") would make him the first living bestselling author the world had ever seen. Luther did not realize the power of the printing press and then start publishing. Instead, he was as surprised as anyone that his little German sermon became such a "hit" but then realized what an important tool this would be for spreading Wittenberg's witness to the gospel.

Second, the *Sermon* already included Luther's reactions to his very earliest opponents. Johann Tetzel, thinking himself personally attacked in the *Ninety-Five Theses*, worked in January with Conrad Wimpina (c. 1465-1531), professor of theology at the University of Frankfurt/Oder, and at a meeting of the Saxon Dominicans there defended printed theses against Luther's on 20 January 1518, receiving a doctorate in theology as a result. In addition to responding to Tetzel in his *Explanations of the Ninety-Five Theses*, published in August 1518, Luther also touched on some of Tetzel's arguments in the *Sermon*. Tetzel, in turn, responded in German to the *Sermon*, in a publication that was *never* reprinted.[16]

Third, and perhaps most striking, the *Sermon* contains no reference to papal authority *at all*. This strongly suggests that Luther's earliest concern was not to attack Rome but instead to instruct, admonish, and comfort laypeople whom he thought misled by the bad theology of the indulgence preachers and the *Summary Instruction*. By 12-14 October 1518, when the papal legate Cajetan interviewed Luther in Augsburg, the question of papal authority had become far more important—to be heightened even further by the Leipzig debates with Johann Eck (1486-1543) in the summer of 1519. But at this early juncture, the *Sermon* again reveals the heart of Luther's concern: bad preaching and theology and what it does to the faithful. And it shows Luther's remarkable ability to use the German language to transform the complicated Latin debates of the scholars into plain language for all to understand. A letter from Pope Leo X to Cajetan, dated August 23 1518, included complaints about Luther's German writings and

16. Johann Tetzel, *Rebuttal against Luther's Sermon on Indulgences and Grace*, trans. Dewey Weiss Kramer (Atlanta: Pitts Theology Library, 2012). Luther then answered this response with *Eine Freiheit des Sermons päpstlichen Ablaß und Gnad belangend* (1518) in: WA 1:380-93. It was reprinted eleven times.

revealed that even his opponents were realizing the importance of those documents and the "public opinion" that they shaped.

Looking Back

These three very different writings—academic theses, a formal letter, and a popular sermon—reveal three central foci of the Reformation. It was an academic event in that Luther, a professor of theology, wanted to open up a scholarly discussion about indulgences. It was an ecclesiastical event, in that Luther sent these theses to the Archbishop of Mainz in order to challenge him to rein in the worst abuses of the current preaching of the plenary "Peter's indulgence" by Johann Tetzel. And it was a pastoral event, demonstrated most clearly in Luther's sermon designed to instruct the people in the dangers of confusing indulgences with God's grace.

What do these three documents tell us about Martin Luther's theology and the origins of the Reformation? First and foremost, Luther chief concern and the heart of what one scholar has aptly named the "unexpected Reformation,"[17] was the reform of preaching and what bad preaching does to the faithful. In the *Ninety-Five Theses*, the Letter to Albrecht, and the *Sermon on Indulgences and Grace* the same theme runs throughout: The chief threat to the Christian church occurs when its leaders and preachers leave the people to their own devices for avoiding God's works of judgment and forgiveness.

Second, and equally important, Luther was convinced that believers could not buy their way around the law and judgment of God. The point of Christian piety was not to escape "mortification" (Rom. 8:13; Col. 3:5) by purchasing indulgences. Instead, only by putting to death of the old creature does the new creature of faith in God's promises come to life. From his own experience as a preacher

---

17. Heiko Augustinus Oberman, *Luther: Man between God and the Devil* (New Haven: Yale University Press, 1989), 111-206.

of a dedication indulgence and in listening to his people's interpretation of the message of indulgence preachers like Tetzel, Luther realized that indulgences had become a means of escaping God's judgment through works or even purchasing exemptions and that they thus worked completely against true sorrow for sin (contrition).

Third, in the *Ninety-Five Theses* Luther also raised questions about the "treasury of merits" and insisted (against the papal decree of Clement VI) that this treasury was not indulgences but (thesis 58) "the gospel of the grace and glory of God." This contradiction of a papal decree, which he admitted knowing about at the time he wrote the *Ninety-Five Theses*, would bring him into direct conflict with the authority of the pope, as his interview in Augsburg with the pope's representative Cardinal Cajetan made clear.[18] But it also hinted at the other side of Luther's theology that otherwise barely comes to expression in these documents: the nature of the gospel itself.

As demonstrated above, the unconditional nature of God's mercy (the heart of the gospel) was *not* the focus of the initial dispute over indulgences but rather attempts to purchase an exemption from God's judgment were. As Luther made far clearer in his *Explanations of the Ninety-Five Theses* from 1518, however, his understanding of the nature of the gospel undergirded his objections to indulgences. Not only was the gospel the true treasure of the church (thesis 58), but in an earlier thesis (7) Luther defines how and where a person hears the gospel, namely in the confessional from the priest. When the priest (or even the pope) removes the guilt of sin by pronouncing a penitent forgiven, that is gospel. Here is the way he put it in theses 6 and 7: "The pope cannot remit any guilt except by declaring and confirming its remission by God. . . . God remits

---

18. Martin Luther, *Proceedings at Augsburg* (1518), in *The Annotated Luther, vol. 1: The Roots of Reform*, ed. Timothy J. Wengert (Minneapolis: Fortress, 2015), 128-65.

the guilt of absolutely no one unless at the same time God subjects in all things the one humbled to the God's vicar, the priest." This declaration (thesis 6) and its humble acceptance (thesis 7), rather than the satisfying of punishment, were for Luther the central thing in penance.

By the time the *Explanations of the Ninety-Five Theses* were published in August 1518, Luther had come to express the ramifications of these statements far more boldly. In his explanation of thesis 7, he first clarified the nature of justification. "So it seems to me, and I declare: When God begins to justify a person, he first of all condemns him or her. The one he wishes to raise up, he destroys; the one whom he wishes to heal, he smites; and the one to whom he wishes to give life, he kills. . . ."[19] The movement from law, which condemns, to gospel, which gives life, is unmistakable. But for Luther justification is neither giving lip service to a doctrine *about* forgiveness nor simply feeling bad about having sinned but is rather an announcement of forgiveness that brings the hearer to trust that very announcement. So he adds:

> Persons who are to be absolved must guard themselves very carefully from any doubt that God has remitted their sins, in order that they may find peace of heart. For although they are uncertain regarding the anguish of their conscience (as must always be the case if it is a true sorrow), nevertheless they are constrained to abide by the judgment of another [the priest declaring forgiveness]—not at all on account of the priest himself or his power, but on account of the word of Christ who cannot lie. . . . This peace, therefore, is that sweetest power, for which, from the depth of our hearts, we ought to give the greatest thanks to God, who has given such power to mortals—that power which is the only consolation for sins and for wretched consciences, if only people will believe that which Christ has promised is true.[20]

19. LW 31:99, with slight revisions.
20. LW 31:100-01, with slight revisions.

Here, finally, Luther elucidates the contours of his insight into the nature of justification by faith alone. When the priest declares a person forgiven, that very unconditional declaration of freedom from guilt becomes true for that person only when believing that it is "for me." Otherwise, if one doubts, then the very gift God in Christ wants to bestow, while valid, is finally not effective. Luther's opponents, such as Cajetan, would insist that such certainty of faith was simply a form of spiritual pride, so that a person in the confessional needed to be humble by expressing uncertainty about whether God's promises of forgiveness applied directly to them. Luther realized that this kind of humility was simply a human work designed to make God's promise depend not on God's mercy but on human striving.

1

The Ninety-Five Theses

The *Ninety-Five Theses* of Martin Luther may constitute one of the best known and yet least understood of his writings. Given the terseness of individual theses, the technical nature of many of the arguments and the debates over the history of the document, this is hardly surprising. In addition to the overview of penance and indulgences in the volume introduction, a twenty-first-century reader needs to consider certain other historical and literary aspects of the document.

Historical Considerations

By the Late Middle Ages indulgences had become a central part of piety for many people in the Western Church but were also a useful means of financial support for a cash-strapped papacy, so that indulgence preaching was labeled a *sacrum negotium* (holy business). When Leo X proclaimed a plenary "Peter's Indulgence" in 1515, the stated reason was to raise money to rebuild the Basilica of Sts.

Peter and Paul in Rome. Half of the money raised, however, was to go to the Augsburg banking family, the Fuggers, in order to pay a debt owed by Archbishop Albrecht of Brandenburg, as described in the introduction. The religious benefits attached to the indulgence were surely also part of Albrecht's concern. In any case, at the time of writing the *Ninety-Five Theses* Luther knew nothing of these financial dealings.

To proclaim this indulgence Albrecht settled upon the well-known Dominican preacher, Johann Tetzel (1465-1519), and he asked his court theologians to prepare a booklet, the *Summary Instruction*, which described the limits and benefits of this indulgence for potential preachers.[1] Some of Luther's objections in the *Ninety-Five Theses* arose from this source and from Tetzel's preaching, some of which likely overstepped the boundaries of the *Summary Instruction*. According to contemporary accounts and pictures, he would have been met at a town's gates by all the important government and church officials, who would have processed to the town' main church where the papal coat-of-arms and the papal bull[2] decreeing this indulgence would be prominently displayed, while all the organs and bells in the town's churches sounded. All other preaching would be halted so that the citizenry had opportunity to give full attention to Tetzel and the indulgences he had to offer.

Although banned from electoral Saxony, Tetzel set up shop around the edges of electoral Saxony where Wittenberg's citizens could undertake the short journey to purchase this religiously valuable

---

1. This included threats to any who impeded preaching this indulgence, the invalidation of previous indulgences, the necessity for building St. Peter's in Rome, the promise of complete remission of all temporal penalties here and in Purgatory, the sliding scale of payment depending on one's station in life, a confessional letter instructing the confessor to forgive all sins (which could be used twice—including at the time of death), participation of oneself and one's dead relatives in the "goods" of the church (especially its prayers and other good works) and remission of penalties for souls in purgatory.
2. A technical term for an official papal bulletin or message.

blessing. Those who purchased such certificates began showing them to their priests at home, including to Martin Luther, Augustinian friar and preacher at St. Mary's, the city church in Wittenberg, and describing Tetzel's preaching.

Besides his own uncertainty about indulgences, Luther encountered uncertainty and complaints about indulgences from laypersons and rumors about exaggerations in Tetzel's indulgence preaching.[3] Then, having obtained a copy of the *Summary Instruction*, he began serious investigation concerning the nature of indulgences in the summer of 1517, researching the books of Canon Law[4] and asking experts for their assistance. What this study revealed to Luther was that the ancient church had understood the satisfaction owed for temporal punishment of sin quite differently than the church of his day and, in his opinion, that the pope had authority over and, thus, could offer indulgences *only* for ecclesiastical punishment established in canon law, which had nothing to do with divine punishment.

For the debate over the posting and distribution of the *Ninety-Five Theses*, see the volume introduction. In addition to sending copies to the archbishop of Mainz on 31 October 1517 and at nearly the same time to the bishop of Brandenburg, it is also certain that Luther sent copies of the *Theses* to his friends, including Johannes Lang (ca. 1487-1548), where in a letter dated 11 November 1517, Luther asked for Lang's feedback.[5] Luther's later recollections of these times occasionally single out 31 October. In the November letter to Lang, Luther simply passed along the theses as to a friend (apologizing for not having sent them sooner). This reflected the fact that, as he stated in his introduction to the *Ninety-Five Theses*, Luther expected people

---

3. See LW 51:26-31.
4. A collection of binding church decrees from councils and popes assembled beginning in the twelfth century by Gratian (active ca. 1150) and commented upon by professors of church law in the centuries following.
5. WA Br 1:121-23.

from a distance to respond by letter—a unique request regarding theses for debate. Scholars agree that no public disputation ever took place, as Luther later admitted, although the faculty of the University of Mainz, to which the archbishop gave responsibility to judge Luther's theses, assumed in their judgment of December 1517 that such a disputation must have taken place, as would normally have occurred in such cases.

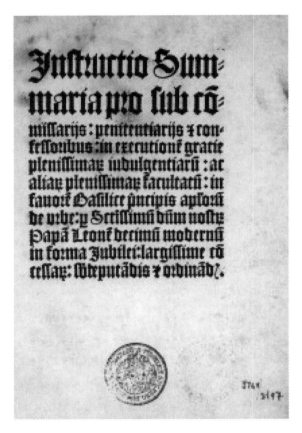

Fig. 1.1 Summary Instruction.

Even if Luther did print and post the *Theses* for debate, he had no notion what the results of such a debate would be and certainly did not have in mind attacking the papacy and certainly not splitting the church—something he never claimed to have done in any case. Indeed, in letters from early 1518, Luther seemed rather surprised at how widely the *Theses* had been disseminated. Luther wrote and distributed the theses as a matter of pastoral and theological concern, showing every respect for his ecclesiastical superiors by informing and warning them of the *Theses'* content.

Literary Considerations

Luther clearly composed the *Ninety-Five Theses* as theses for debate. Yet, when compared to other theses that he and other professors were composing at around the same time, the *Ninety-Five Theses* contain some turns that were decidedly not intended for classroom debate using logic and syllogisms. They have a far more rhetorical flare than one finds in other university theses, both before and after 1517. Indeed, it may help to consider this document as a mixture of logical argument and impassioned speech, as Luther addresses what he viewed as a looming pastoral and theological problem in the church. His defense of the *Theses* published in the summer of 1518 contains lengthy arguments, gleaned from Scripture, the church fathers, papal decrees, and canon law, and thus takes the form of an academic debate.[6] But the *Theses* themselves, the letter to Albrecht, and the *Sermon on Indulgences and Grace* aim at both the head and the heart of the reader (although Luther would hardly have made the same distinction between the two that today's readers do).

As an example of a tightly constructed logical argument, there are the first four theses, which briefly outline Luther's assumptions about the nature of penitence.[7] Similarly, theses 5-20 provide a focused argument about the limits of papal authority in giving indulgence.

6. LW 31: 77-252.
7. Throughout Luther's works, in both Latin and German, as single word (*poenitentia* and *Buße*), may be best rendered Penance, penitence or repentance, depending on the context.

Again, theses 56-68 address the single question of the nature of the "treasury of merits," which Luther argued had not been well understood in the church. Yet even these sections of the *Ninety-Five Theses* contain certain rhetorical turns of phrase that are unusual and thus worth noting.

As a student at the University of Erfurt in the early 1500s, Luther would have learned the basics of constructing and ornamenting writings according to the rhetorical rules current in his day.[8] One began with an exordium, designed to get the reader's attention and favor. Then a narration of the accepted facts or presuppositions followed. A succinct description of the subject under discussion (sometimes labeled the "state of the controversy" or simply "theme") was followed by what was always the longest part of any speech or writing, the confirmation, which sought to prove the various parts of the author's argument. A so-called confutation, which anticipated opponents' objections and rebutted them, was followed by the peroration, a conclusion that either summarized the author's point or once again appealed to the reader's good will in taking the arguments to heart.[9] One hint that Luther was also thinking rhetorically comes from the *Explanations of the Ninety-Five Theses*, where Luther labels theses 81-91 a confutation. The theses that follow (92-95) are clearly an open appeal to the readers and form an obvious peroration. They have such a high rhetorical tone that several of Luther's opponents ignore them altogether.

Based upon the presence of these more explicitly rhetorical parts, one can also detect the rhetorical structure of other sections of the

---

8. For Luther's use of rhetoric, see Birgit Stolt *Martin Luthers Rhetorik des Herzens* (Tübingen: Mohr Siebeck, 2000); Neil R. Leroux, *Luther's Rhetoric: Strategies and Style from the Invocavit Sermons* (St. Louis: Concordia, 2002); Helmar Junghans, *Martin Luther und die Rhetorik* (Leipzig: Hirzel, 1998).

9. The Latin terms, some already found in Cicero and Quintilian, were *exordium, narratio, status controversiae, confirmatio, confutatio,* and *peroratio*.

Theses. The announcement of the debate functions as an **exordium**, asks for the reader's attention and response for the sake of the truth and invokes Christ's blessing. The first four theses, as Luther later insists in his *Explanations*, were not up for debate but represented the underlying assumptions on which the entire writing rested and thus functioned as a **narration**. The fifth thesis, by contrast, states precisely **the heart of the controversy**: "The pope neither desires nor is able to remit any penalties except those imposed by his own authority or that of the canons." That Luther includes the word "desires" here is a further indication of the rhetorical, emotive side to these *Theses*. The determination of papal desires was hardly a matter of syllogisms and logical arguments. In line with the centrality of this thesis, the *Explanations* insisted that this was the first debatable thesis.

What follows in theses 6-80 contains the proof or **confirmation**, rhetorically speaking, for thesis 5. Here Luther addresses the central topic of the limits of papal authority to remove the penalty (though not the guilt) of a person's sin (theses 6-20). Thesis 20, introduced by "therefore," summarizes the foregoing arguments in language echoing thesis five. In thesis 21 he mentions for the first time the indulgence preachers and begins the first of three corollaries to his main point: theses 21-40 reject bad preaching and its false claims;[10] theses 41-55 discuss how Christians ought to be taught given the tension between preaching indulgences and encouraging truly Christian works and the gospel;[11] and theses 56-68 define the treasures of the church again over against the claims of indulgence

10. This first corollary has three parts: preaching release from all penalties is wrong (21-24); the papal relation to the souls in purgatory (25-29); the relation of contrition to indulgence preaching (30-40).
11. This corollary explores proper preaching and employs the rhetorically charged phrase, "Christians are to be taught." After introducing the theme (40), a first section deals with wealth, almsgiving, and the problem of false trust (42-52), and a second, smaller section contrasts indulgences to the gospel (53-55).

preachers. A final section (69–80) outlines the proper response church leaders should take to restrain such preachers.

What Luther later labels the **confutation** (81–91) possesses its own rhetorical cleverness, in that, instead of providing objections to his *own* argument that favored narrowing indulgences to the lifting of ecclesiastical penalties, Luther introduces the character of a sharp layperson, whose objections to the reigning view of indulgences have (in Luther's mind) no answers except by returning to Luther's simple solution (thesis 91), which (like thesis 5) is connected to "the spirit and intention of the pope." Many of these objections may be found in the writings of others before 1517. Luther's conclusion, or **peroration** (92–95), contains some of the most rhetorically charged language of the entire piece, applying the condemnation of the prophet Jeremiah to the indulgence preachers, who falsely imagine they are offering peace, and contrasting it to the proper preaching of the cross. The final two theses match the argument at the very beginning of the tract, that the entire life of the Christian is one of penitence.

Themes

Because of the form of Luther's argument (using tightly worded theses to express his point) and because of the foreign nature of the debate itself, it is often hard to understand the *Theses* and the effect that they had on those first readers. Paying attention to the structure of the *Theses* helps to identify several different important points. First and foremost, Luther had indulgence preachers in mind while writing, as the cover letter to Archbishop Albrecht also made clear. References to their abuses appear throughout the theses. At the same time, Luther's research into the nature of indulgences had driven him to the conclusion that their original meaning had become obscured by later practices, especially by the confusion of penalties imposed by the church for the sake of discipline with punishments meted out by God (thesis 5). But his research had also led him to Erasmus's commentary on the New Testament, and so Luther argued that the entire life of the Christian is one of penitence (theses 1-4).

On this basis, he also argued that the present practice surrounding indulgences, which gave the pope authority over God's punishment of sinners on earth and in purgatory, actually harms the Christian in preventing the move from the death of the sinner to life in God's promises. (See thesis 5 and the proofs in 6-7 on the removal of guilt and 8-20 on the nature of punishment in this life and in purgatory). On this basis, he then attacks what he sees as the exaggerated claims of the indulgence preachers, who promised forgiveness to those who purchased the letters for themselves and release from purgatory for those who purchased them for their deceased loved ones (theses 21ff.). After providing the content of proper preaching (theses 41-51, with their refrain, "Christians are to be taught"), Luther summarizes what he saw as other exaggerations by these preachers (theses 52-55) and then examines a related problem of the "treasury of the church," from which, it had been claimed, the pope could apply to sinners the merits of Christ and the saints through indulgences. Having rejected other definitions, Luther insists that this treasury was none other than the gospel itself (theses 56-67), and he concludes with a plea to bishops and others to rein in these preachers (theses 68-80). After listing the sharp objections of the laity, Luther ends with an emotion-laden conclusion, contrasting the false peace offered Christians through indulgences to the cross of Christ and, hence, the Christian life of continual penitence.

Reactions

The *Ninety-Five Theses* elicited immediate reaction from several different groups and individuals. First, Luther's friends in Nuremberg and elsewhere saw to its wider distribution throughout the Holy Roman Empire by printing the document. Individuals, especially people associated with Renaissance humanism, regarded this as a further step in the renewal of good theology on the basis of ancient sources.[12] Those in Wittenberg also supported Luther's position, especially Luther's colleague Andreas Bodenstein from Karlstadt (1486-1541), who soon entered the lists in attacking Johann Eck.

But Luther's appeal to Archbishop Albrecht resulted in the cardinal sending the theses to his own theological faculty in Mainz for their judgment and to the papal court. Near the end of 1517, the former published a rejection of Luther's claims. The response from Rome, which was entrusted to Sylvester Prierias, the papal court theologian, was published by the summer of 1518.[13] Meanwhile, in January 1518 Johann Tetzel received his doctorate at the University of Frankfurt/Oder defending theses composed by Conrad Wimpina, all of which attacked Luther's theses. A few months later, in March or April, Tetzel published another fifty theses, each one using Luther's own pointed phrase ("Christians must be taught").[14] Luther responded in part to Tetzel in his German *Sermon on Indulgences and Grace*, going into even more detail in his *Explanations*.[15] Meanwhile, Johann Eck from the University of Ingolstadt had also gotten hold of a copy of the *95 Theses* and wrote a response that he shared in manuscript form with some friends. When Luther received a copy of these *Obelisks*

---

12. See the classic arguments by Lewis Spitz, *The Protestant Reformation: 1517-1559* (New York: Harper & Row, 1985), 88-101.

13. Luther replied in his *Response to the Dialogue of Silvester Prierias concerning the Power of the Pope* (1518), in WA 1:644-86, with 9:782-86.

14. Both are contained in Peter Fabisch and Erwin Iserloh, eds., *Dokumente zur Causa Lutheri (1517-1521)*, vol. 1: *Das Gutachten des Prierias und weitere Schriften gegen Luthers Ablaßthesen (1517-1518)* (Münster: Aschendorff, 1988), 310-37 (*Frankfurter Thesen*) and 363-375 (*Fünfzig Positiones*).

15. See below, pp. 41-48, and, for the *Explanations*, LW 31:77-252.

(so-called because Eck had marked each objection to Luther's theses with an obelisk [†]), he felt betrayed, since just the year before he had attempted to begin correspondence with Eck. He published a response, called the *Asterisks*, in which he answered line-for-line Eck's objections, using an asterisk (*) to mark his own arguments. By October 1518, when Luther traveled to Augsburg for an interview with Cardinal Cajetan, the arguments had begun to move beyond the original issue of indulgences and their preaching and on to other topics, especially the authority of the pope, which all of Luther's opponents believed Luther had attacked as well.[16] Nevertheless, several later judgments by the Universities of Louvain and Paris, and an extensive refutation by the French theologian, Jacobus Latomus (c. 1475-1544), also formed part of the initial reaction to the *Theses*.[17] By the time Johann Eck squared off with Karlstadt and Luther for the Leipzig debates in the summer of 1519, the central issue in Luther's case had become the authority of the papacy and church councils in relation to the Word of God.

Whatever Luther may have expected to result from the *Theses* had taken an unexpected (and, perhaps, unwanted) turn, one that was light years from the original debate. Nevertheless, when Johann Eck arrived in Rome in 1520, bent on writing a papal bull of excommunication for Luther, at least some of the "heretical" doctrines came from the *Ninety-Five Theses* and its defense.[18] At the same time, Luther continued to find a variety of supporters throughout the Holy Roman Empire. While Erasmus of Rotterdam (1466-1536) and others remained somewhat distant and finally antagonistic or only praised Luther for his courage to stand up to the

---

16. For the interview with Cajetan, see, *The Annotated Luther, vol. 1: The Roots of Reform*, ed. Timothy J. Wengert (Minneapolis: Fortress, 2015), 121-65.
17. See Luther's response, *Against Latomus* (1521), in LW 32:133-260.
18. See Luther's *Defense and Explanation of All the Articles* (1521) in LW 32:3-99.

authorities of the day, still others found his thought quite convincing. These included Martin Bucer [1591-1551], the future reformer of Strasbourg, and Johannes Brenz, reformer of Schwäbisch Hall and later of Württemberg.

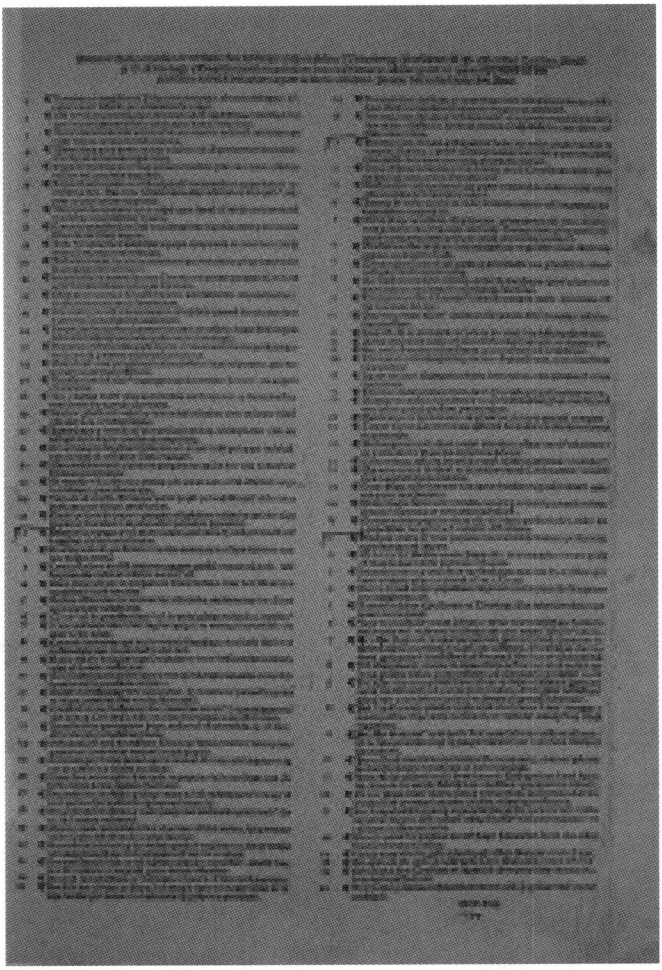

Fig. 1.2 Image of 95 Theses.

[The Ninety-Five Theses or] Disputation for Clarifying the Power of Indulgences[19]

Out of love and zeal for bringing the truth to light, what is written below will be debated in Wittenberg with the Reverend Father Martin Luther,[20] Master of Arts and Sacred Theology and regularly appointed lecturer on these subjects at that place, presiding. Therefore, he requests that those who cannot be present to discuss orally with us will in their absence do so by letter.[21] In the name of our Lord Jesus Christ. Amen.

1. Our Lord and Master Jesus Christ, in saying "Do penance … ,"[22] wanted the entire life of the faithful to be one of penitence.

2. This phrase cannot be understood as referring to sacramental Penance,[23] that is, confession and satisfaction as administered by the clergy.[24]

3. Yet it does not mean solely inner penitence—indeed such inner

---

19. This translation is based upon that of Charles M. Jacobs, revised by Harold J. Grimm in LW 31:17–33, as well as upon WA 1:233–38, also referring to helpful notes in MLStA 1:171–85. The title is taken from the 1518 Basel reprint.
20. Or, in two printings, *Lutther*. Around this time, he began spelling his name "Luther" in his letters, in part as a play on the Greek word, *eleutherius* ("the free one"). See WA Br 1:122 (letter to Johannes Lang [c. 1487–1548], dated 11 November 1517) and LW 48:55 (letter to Georg Spalatin [1484–1545], dated 18 January 1518).
21. There is no evidence that such a public debate took place in Wittenberg. Their publication and subsequent distribution led to vigorous debate. This functions as a kind of exordium to the entire document. See above, pp. 5–8.
22. Luther is quoting the standard Vulgate rendering of Matt. 4:17 (*Poenitentiam agite*, translated "Repent!" in most English versions). In Latin and German, however, the phrase may be rendered "Do penance," "Be penitent," or "Repent." These first four theses represent the basic narration of what Luther considered generally accepted facts.
23. As the *Explanations of the Ninety-Five Theses* (1518), LW 31:83f., made clear, Luther was relying here on Erasmus's annotations to the Greek text, first published in 1516, which pointed out that the Greek verb *metanoeite* did not mean "do penance" but "come to one's senses" and thus did not refer to the sacrament of penance.
24. For the parts of the sacrament of penance (contrition, confession, and satisfaction) and the distinction between guilt and punishment, see the introduction, p. xvii. Luther touched on contrition in thesis 3 and punishment (*poena*) in thesis 4.

penitence is nothing unless it outwardly produces various mortifications of the flesh.[25]

4. And thus,[26] penalty[27] remains as long as hatred of self[28] (that is, true inner penitence) remains, namely, until our entrance into the kingdom of heaven.[29]

5. The pope neither desires nor is able to remit[30] any penalties except those imposed by his own discretion or that of the canons.[31]

6. The pope cannot remit any guilt except by declaring and confirming its remission by God or, of course, by remitting guilt in [legal] cases reserved to himself.[32] In showing contempt regarding such cases, the guilt would certainly remain.

7. God remits the guilt of absolutely no one unless at the same time God subjects in all things the one humbled to God's vicar, the priest.[33]

8. The penitential canons[34] were imposed only on the living, and,

---

25. Inward penitence is contrition. External putting to death of the flesh was part of satisfaction. For the medieval debate over when God's grace was infused in the penitent (at the moment of contrition or in confessional), see the introduction, p. xvii.

26. Latin: *itaque*. These theses consisted in a series of logical arguments, so that this concludes the underlying narrative for the actual disputation.

27. Latin: *poena*, the root of *poeni-tentia*. The linguistic and theological connection between penalty and penance is hard to capture in English.

28. See John 12:25.

29. See Matt. 7:21-23. That is, until after death.

30. That is, set aside or forgive.

31. Thesis 5 states Luther's central premise. Old church law had specified that penalties (*poena*) for sin be imposed before absolution was administered (see thesis 12) and were part of church discipline. Hence, Luther argues that the church could show leniency, or indulgence, only in regard to these ecclesiastical penalties, not God's punishment. See the introduction, pp. xv-xxi. The phrase "by his discretion or that of the canons" was a technical term describing how a priest in the confession would first see if the sin in question had a penalty prescribed in the penitential canons and, if not, could use his discretion.

32. In terms of divine grace and the removal of guilt (*culpa*), priests simply announced God's forgiveness. Regarding especially heinous sins, ecclesiastical absolution was restricted to the papal see.

33. In the *Explanations* (1518) of this thesis, LW 31:99, Luther emphasizes how God moves the penitent from condemnation (law) to absolution (gospel). In October 1518, Cardinal Cajetan rejected Luther's position about certainty, as expressed in the *Explanations* (31:100), that "the person who is to be absolved must guard himself very carefully from any doubt that God has remitted his sins, in order that he may find peace of heart."

34. These rules, contained in medieval penitential books, were derived from the practices of the

according to the canons themselves, nothing should be imposed on those about to die.[35]

9. Accordingly, the Holy Spirit through the pope acts in a kindly manner toward us in papal decrees by always exempting the moment of death and the case of necessity.[36]

10. Those priests act ignorantly and wickedly who, in the case of the dying, reserve canonical penalties for one's time in purgatory.

11. Those "tares" about changing the canonical penalty into the penalty of purgatory certainly seem to have been "sown" while the bishops "were sleeping."[37]

12. Formerly, canonical penalties were imposed not after, but before absolution, as tests of true contrition.[38]

13. Through death, those about to die are absolved of all [such penalties] and are already dead as far as canon laws are concerned, in that by right they have release from them.[39]

14. Imperfect purity or love on the part of the dying person necessarily brings with it great fear. The smaller the love, the greater the fear.

15. This fear or horror is enough by itself alone (to say nothing of other things) to constitute the penalty of purgatory, since it is very near the horror of despair.[40]

---

ancient church for imposing ecclesiastical penalties on flagrant sinners, in order to reconcile them to the church. See above, pp. xvii–xviii.

35. Given that the church's juridical authority ended at death. See also thesis 13.

36. These two exceptions may be found throughout canon law. See MLStA 1:177, nn.20–21.

37. Luther is referring to the parable of the wheat and tares (sown by the evil one while the owner slept) from Matt. 13:25. Already John Chrysostom (c. 347–407) in his homilies on Matthew (XLVI) had connected those who sleep with ecclesiastical rulers. Throughout the *Theses*, Luther distinguished between canonical (ecclesiastical) penalties and penalties imposed by God in purgatory.

38. See above, n. 34.

39. See theses 8–10.

40. This association of terror with the punishment of purgatory, already found among German mystics like Johannes Tauler (c. 1300–1361), is central to Luther's experience of the cross and attacks on his faith. See the *Explanations* (1518), LW 31:125–30.

16. It seems that hell, purgatory, and heaven differ from each other as much as despair, near despair, and assurance.[41]

17. It seems necessary that, for souls in purgatory, as the horror decreases so love increases.[42]

18. It neither seems proved—either by any logical arguments or by Scripture—that souls in purgatory are outside a state of merit,[43] that is, unable to grow in love;

19. nor does it seem to be proved that these souls, at least not all of them, are certain and assured of their own salvation—even though we ourselves are completely certain about [their destiny].

20. Therefore,[44] the pope understands by the phrase "plenary[45] remission of all penalties" not actually "all penalties" but only "penalties imposed by himself."

21. And so,[46] those indulgence preachers err who say that through the pope's indulgences a person is released[47] and saved from every penalty.

22. On the contrary, to souls in purgatory he remits no penalty that they should have paid[48] in this life according to canon law.

23. If any remission of all penalties whatsoever could be granted to anyone, it would certainly be granted only to the most perfect, that is, to the very fewest.

---

41. Latin: *securitas*. Security often had a negative connotation in the Middle Ages, but here Luther uses it to describe the complete assurance of the soul in heaven.

42. Luther had stated a similar view in his lectures on Romans (1515–1516), LW 25:381f. For earlier discussions over whether a soul is active or passive in purgatory, see Thomas Aquinas (*Commentary on the Sentences*, bk. IV d. 45, q. 2, a. 1), who came to the opposite conclusion.

43. That is, a state of grace as opposed to a state of sin.

44. Latin: *igitur*. This concludes the argument in the previous theses (6–19) and reiterates the point in thesis 5.

45. I.e., "full."

46. Latin: *itaque*. This introduces a first corollary (theses 21–40) to Luther's just-concluded main argument and begins an attack on indulgence preachers, focusing on preaching release from all penalties, the limits of papal authority, and the nature of contrition.

47. Latin: *solvere*.

48. Latin: *solvere*.

24. Because of this, most people are inevitably deceived by means of this indiscriminate and high-sounding promise of release from penalty.

25. The kind of power that a pope has over purgatory in general corresponds to the power that any bishop or local priest[49] has in particular in his diocese or parish.[50]

26. The pope does best in that he grants remission to souls [in purgatory] not by "the power of the keys," which he does not possess [here], but "by way of intercession."[51]

27. They "preach human opinions"[52] who say that, as soon as a coin thrown into the money chest clinks, a soul flies out [of purgatory].[53]

28. It is certain that when a coin clinks in the money chest profits and avarice may well be increased, but the intercession of the church rests on God's choice alone.

29. Who knows whether all the souls in purgatory want to be redeemed, given what is recounted about St. Severinus and St. Paschasius?[54] [55]

---

49. Latin: *curatus*, the particular priest serving a parish.
50. Luther's second argument against the indulgence preachers (theses 25–29) aims at their exaggerated claims about releasing souls from purgatory.
51. Luther is arguing that the "power of the keys," given to Peter (Matt. 16:19) and, by extension, to all priests and bishops to forgive sin, did not extend to purgatory but that only intercession did. *Per modum suffragii* (by way of intercession) was a technical term when one intercedes with prayers and in other ways especially for souls in purgatory (for example, through masses for their souls). Some medieval theologians, including Bonaventure (1221–1274), had suggested that this was the basis for the papal authority to grant indulgences. Luther discusses this more fully in the other document enclosed with Albrecht's letter, the so-called *Tractate on Indulgences*.
52. Plato (c. 428–c. 347 bce), *Theaetetus*, 170.
53. Perhaps a phrase used by Johann Tetzel (see Luther's Letter to Archbishop Albrecht below, p. 33), as he admitted in his attack on the *Ninety-Five Theses*. The German ditty, "As soon as money in the chest rings, a soul from purgatory springs," predated Tetzel and was used commonly to sell indulgences.
54. Latin: *Paschalius*. Luther also referred to such legends somewhat more skeptically in the *Explanations* (1518), LW 31:178.
55. Severinus, archbishop of Cologne (late fourth century), and Paschasius, deacon of Rome (fifth century), preferred to remain longer in purgatory to gain greater glory in heaven, according to Luther's source, Johann von Paltz (1445–1511), a theologian at the University of Erfurt when Luther studied there, who mentioned both saints in his *Supplementum Coelifodinae* (Erfurt,

30. No one is secure in the genuineness of one's own contrition—much less in having attained "plenary remission."[56]

31. As rare as a person who is truly penitent, just so rare is someone who truly acquires indulgences; indeed, the latter is the rarest of all.[57]

32. Those who believe that they can be secure in their salvation through indulgence letters will be eternally damned along with their teachers.

33. One must especially beware of those who say that those indulgences of the pope are "God's inestimable gift" by which a person is reconciled to God.[58]

34. For these indulgent graces are only based upon the penalties of sacramental satisfaction instituted by human beings.[59]

35. Those who teach that contrition is not necessary on the part of those who would rescue souls [from purgatory] or who would buy confessional privileges[60] do not preach Christian views.

36. Any truly remorseful Christian has a right to full remission of guilt and penalty,[61] even without indulgence letters.

37. Any true Christian, living or dead, possesses a God-given share

---

1504), E 6v, and made the same misspelling. Paltz based his comments about Paschasius on Pope Gregory I (c. 540–604), *Dialogues*, bk. 4, ch. 40 and about Severinus on Peter Damian (c. 1007–1072/73), *De variis miraculosis narrationibus*, ch. 5 (MPL 145:578).

56. This begins a third argument against bad preaching, foreshadowed in the saying in thesis 27. Luther connects assurance to God's promise. Luther quotes a technical term used in the *Summary Instruction*, which connects the Peter's indulgence to *complete* forgiveness of sin (i.e., guilt and punishment). In the *Explanations* (1518), LW 31:178f., Luther claims to be using the language of the indulgence preachers, who insisted that the benefits of indulgences were tied to genuine contrition.

57. Here "penitence" is understood as contrition and "indulgences" as lenience.

58. This addresses another claim of indulgence preachers (see theses 21, 27), also found in the *Summary Instruction*.

59. See above, thesis 5.

60. Latin: *confessionalia*. Such letters allowed penitents to choose their own confessors and were specifically mentioned in the *Summary Instruction* that defined the Peter's Indulgence. Luther again touches on this in thesis 84.

61. See the introduction, p. 7. In Advent sermons of 1516 and Lenten sermons in 1517 (published in early 1517), Johann von Staupitz (c. 1460–1524), the head of Luther's order in Germany, had made a similar point.

in all the benefits[62] of Christ and the church, even without indulgence letters.

38. Nevertheless, remission and participation [in these benefits] from the pope must by no means be despised, because—as I said[63]—they are the declaration of divine remission.

39. It is extremely difficult, even for the most learned theologians, to lift up before the people the liberality of indulgences and the truth about contrition at one and the same time.[64]

40. The "truth about contrition" seeks and loves penalties [for sins]; the "liberality of indulgences" relaxes penalties and at very least gives occasion for hating them.[65]

41. Apostolic indulgences[66] are to be preached with caution, so that the people do not mistakenly think that they are to be preferred to other good works of love.

42. Christians are to be taught[67] that the pope does not intend the acquiring of indulgences to be compared in any way with works of mercy.

43. Christians are to be taught that the one who gives to a poor

---

62. Latin: *participatio omnium bonorum Christi et Ecclesie*, literally "a share in all the goods of Christ and the church." This common technical term (used, for example, by Thomas Aquinas, *Summa Theologica* II/II, d. 63, a. 2, ad 1) encompassed all manner of spiritual blessings.

63. See above, thesis 6.

64. Here and in thesis 40, Luther summarizes the problem of contrition and indulgence preaching, something he himself had also referred to in preaching the anniversary indulgence for the Castle Church in January 1517. Luther also explains this in the so-called *Tract on Indulgences*, attached to the letter to Albrecht. See the introduction, pp. xxiv–xxx.

65. See Luther's comments in a sermon from 24 February 1517, in LW 51:31: "Would that I were a liar when I say that indulgences are rightly so called, for to indulge means to permit, and indulgence is equivalent to impunity, permission to sin, and license to nullify the cross of Christ."

66. That is, indulgences granted by the successor to the apostles, the pope, in this case the so-called Peter's Indulgence. Luther now introduces a second corollary and explores the possibility of good preaching and its relation to good works and the gospel. See also the *Sermon on Indulgences and Grace*, below, p. 45f.

67. This striking phrase, used to introduce theses 42–51, was then borrowed by Tetzel to begin each of his countertheses.

person or lends to the needy[68] does a better deed than if a person acquires indulgences,

44. because love grows through works of love and a person is made better; but through indulgences one is not made better but only freer from penalty [for sin].[69]

45. Christians are to be taught that anyone who sees a destitute person and, while passing such a one by, gives money for indulgences does not buy [gracious] indulgences of the pope but God's wrath.

46. Christians are to be taught that, unless they have more than they need, they must set aside enough for their household and by no means squander it on indulgences.[70]

47. Christians are to be taught that buying indulgences is a matter of free choice, not commanded.[71]

48. Christians are to be taught that the pope, while granting indulgences, needs and thus desires their devout prayer for him more than their money.[72]

49. Christians are to be taught that papal indulgences are useful [for them] only if they do not put their trust in them but extremely harmful if they lose their fear of God because of them.

50. Christians are to be taught that if the pope knew the demands made by the indulgence preachers, he would rather that the Basilica of St. Peter were burned to ashes than that it be constructed using the skin, flesh, and bones of his sheep.[73]

51. Christians are to be taught that the pope ought to give and would want to give of his own wealth—even selling the Basilica of

---

68. See Matt. 5:42.

69. Theses 43 and 44 are, grammatically speaking, one sentence.

70. The Peter's Indulgence was, however, priced on a sliding scale, depending on one's station in life.

71. See below, *Sermon on Indulgences and Grace*, p. 45f.

72. In his letter to Pope Eugene III (d. 1153), bk. 5, Bernard of Clairvaux (1090–1153) describes the importance of the prayers of the faithful in aiding the pope to fulfill his office.

73. For the connection of this papal indulgence to St. Peter's in Rome, see the introduction, pp. xxv–xxvi.

St. Peter if necessary—to those from whom certain declaimers[74] of indulgences are wheedling money.

52. It is vain to trust in salvation by means of indulgence letters, even if the [indulgence] agent—or even the pope himself—were to offer his own soul as security for them.[75]

53. People who forbid the preaching of the Word of God in some churches altogether in order that indulgences may be preached in others are enemies of Christ and the pope.[76]

54. An injustice is done to the Word of God when, in the very same sermon, equal or more time is spent on indulgences than on the Word.[77]

55. It is necessarily the pope's intent that if indulgences, which are a completely insignificant thing, are celebrated with one bell, one procession, and one ceremony, then the gospel, which is the greatest thing of all, should be preached with a hundred bells, a hundred processions, and a hundred ceremonies.[78]

56. The treasures of the church, from which the pope distributes indulgences, are not sufficiently discussed or known among Christ's people.[79]

57. That [these treasures] are not transient worldly[80] riches is certainly clear, because many of the [indulgence] declaimers do not so much freely distribute such riches as only collect them.

58. Nor are they the merits of Christ and the saints, because,

---

74. *Concionatores*: a word for preacher favored by Renaissance humanists and connoting a higher level of oratory, sometimes (as here and in theses 57, 67, and 72) used derogatorily.

75. This summarizes themes brought up in theses 27, 32, and 33 before contrasting preaching of indulgences and the gospel in theses 53–55. The agent (*commisarius*), is the highest authority under whose supervision the indulgence preachers operated.

76. The *Summary Instruction* orders that something like this be done.

77. One version reads: "on the gospel Word."

78. For a description of the ceremonies surrounding indulgence sales, see the introduction, p. 2.

79. Theses 56–68 introduce a third corollary dealing with the unsettled question about the treasury of merits. See the introduction, p. xxi and p. 9.

80. Latin: *temporales*.

even without the pope, these merits always work grace for the inner person and cross, death, and hell for the outer person.[81]

59. St. Laurence said that the poor of the church were the treasures of the church, but he spoke according to the usage of the word "treasure" in his own time.[82]

60. Not without cause, we say that the keys of the church[83] (given by the merits of Christ) are that treasure.

61. For it is clear that the pope's power only suffices for the remission of [ecclesiastical] penalties and for [legal] actions.[84]

62. The true treasure of the church is the most holy gospel of the glory and grace of God.

63. But this treasure is deservedly the most hated, because it makes "the first last."[85]

64. In contrast, the treasure of indulgences is deservedly the most acceptable, because it makes "the last first."

65. Therefore, the treasures of the gospel are nets with which they[86] formerly fished for men of wealth.

66. The treasures of indulgences are nets with which they now fish for the wealth of men.

67. Indulgences, which the declaimers shout about as the greatest "graces," are indeed understood as such—insofar as they promote profits.[87]

---

81. See Luther's lengthy defense in the *Explanations* (1518), LW 31:212–28, which includes reference to the theology of the cross. In the Augsburg interview with Luther in October 1518, Cardinal Cajetan especially objected to this thesis as contradicting the clear teaching of Pope Clement VI (1291–1352). Luther points out that by attaching another's merit to indulgences they cease being truly an indulgence of the church but only another way of paying the same penalty and that such merits work death and life even without papal indulgences.

82. From the *Legenda aurea* [*Golden Legends*] (Strasbourg, 1492): "During these three days Laurence gathered together the poor, lame and blind and carried them into the palace . . . saying, 'Look! These are the eternal treasure . . .'"

83. See above, pp. xix–xxi. Here "the keys" is now a synonym for the gospel of forgiveness.

84. See theses 5–6. In the medieval church, the papal curia was the court of last resort.

85. Matt. 19:30 and 20:16.

86. It is not clear who "they" are—perhaps preachers.

68. Yet they are in truth the least of all when compared to the grace of God and the goodness of the cross.

69. Bishops and parish priests are bound to admit agents[88] of the Apostolic indulgences with all reverence.[89]

70. But all of them are much more bound to strain eyes and ears intently, so that these [agents] do not preach their own daydreams in place of the pope's commission.

71. Let the one who speaks against the truth of the Apostolic indulgences be anathema and accursed,

72. but let the one who guards against the arbitrary and unbridled words used by declaimers of indulgences be blessed.

73. Just as the pope justly thunders against those who, in whatever way they can, contrive to harm the sale of indulgences,[90]

74. much more so does he intend to thunder against those who, under the pretext of indulgences, contrive to harm holy love and the truth.

75. To imagine that papal indulgences are so great that they could absolve a person even for doing the impossible by violating the mother of God is insanity.[91]

76. On the contrary, we have said[92] that papal indulgences cannot take away the very least of venial sins, as far as guilt is concerned.[93]

77. That it is said that even St. Peter, if he were now pope, could not grant greater graces is blasphemy against St. Peter and the pope.

---

87. A play on the word "graces" (*gratiae*), which can also mean "recompense."

88. See above, n. 75.

89. Theses 69–80 introduce a final corollary dealing with the question of proper episcopal oversight for indulgence preachers. See also Luther's *Letter to Albrecht*, p. 33.

90. A reference to threats contained in the *Summary Instruction*.

91. In later writings, Luther attributes the statements in theses 75, 77, and 79 directly to Johann Tetzel, who categorically denied ever saying these things. See *Against Hanswurst* (1541), LW 41:231–35.

92. Especially in theses 5–20. Other versions read: "we say."

93. For the distinction between penalty and guilt and between venial and mortal sins, see the introduction to this volume, pp. xv–xvi.

78. On the contrary, we say that even the present pope, or any pope whatsoever, possesses greater graces—namely, the gospel, "deeds of power, gifts of healing . . ."—as in 1 Cor. 12[:28].

79. To say that the cross, emblazoned with the papal coat-of-arms and erected [in the church where indulgences are preached], is of equal worth to the cross of Christ is blasphemy.[94]

80. The bishops, parish priests, and theologians who allow such sermons free course among the people will have to answer for this.

81. This unbridled preaching makes it difficult even for learned men to defend the reverence due the pope from slander or from the truly sharp questions of the laity:[95]

82. Namely, "Why does the pope not empty purgatory for the sake of the holiest love and the direst need of souls[96] as a matter of the highest justice, given that he redeems countless souls for filthy lucre to build the Basilica [of St. Peter] as a completely trivial matter?"[97]

83. Again, "Why continue funeral and anniversary masses for the dead instead of returning or permitting the withdrawal of the endowments founded for them, since it is against the law to pray for those already redeemed?"[98]

84. Again, "What is this new piety of God and the pope that, for the sake of money, they permit someone who is impious and an enemy to redeem [from purgatory] a pious, God-pleasing soul and

---

94. This was already the argument of Johann von Paltz, *Supplementum*, A 3v, supporting the early sixteenth-century indulgence preacher in Germany, Cardinal Raimund Peraudi (1435–1505), who even preached a plenary indulgence in Erfurt while Luther was a student there.

95. In theses 81–91 Luther examines the consequences of such preaching (see thesis 72) by means of a refutation of objections (*confutatio*), typical in the classical structuring of a speech or writing. See the introduction, pp. 6–8.

96. See thesis 9.

97. The problem of papal avarice was often mentioned in the official complaints (*gravamina*) lodged at imperial diets. See also Luther's *Sermon on Indulgences and Grace*, p. 47.

98. The medieval theologian Gabriel Biel had dealt with this question in relation to masses for baptized children (who were not subject to purgatory). Canon law did not allow prayers for the souls of saints or for the damned.

yet do not, for the sake of the need of that very pious and beloved soul, redeem it purely out of love?"[99]

85. Again, "Why are the penitential canons—long since abrogated and dead in actual fact and through disuse—nevertheless now bought off with money through granting indulgences, as if they were very much alive?"[100]

86. Again, "Why does the pope, whose riches today are more substantial than the richest Crassus,[101] not simply construct the Basilica of St. Peter with his own money rather than with the money of the poor faithful?"

87. Again, "What exactly does the pope 'remit' or 'allow participation in' when it comes to those who through perfect contrition have a right to full remission and a share [in the church's benefits]?"[102]

88. Again, "Could any greater good come to the church than if the pope were to bestow these remissions and participation to each of the faithful a hundred times a day, as he now does but once?"[103]

89. "Since, rather than money, the pope seeks the salvation of souls through indulgences, why does he now suspend the documents and indulgences previously granted, although they have equal efficacy?"[104]

---

99. This objection cannot be found before Luther.

100. Here Luther touches on the question of whether a person could continue to suffer in purgatory for an infraction of canon law now no longer enforced.

101. Latin: *opulentissimis crassis crassiores*, literally "crasser than the richest Crassus," a play on words. Marcus Licinius Crassus (d. 53 bce) was said at one point in life to have owned most of Rome. Luther again is echoing contemporary suspicions about papal wealth.

102. For Luther's sharp layperson, the saints, who through perfect contrition merited complete forgiveness, would not have need for indulgences. This reflected especially the Nominalist emphasis on human ability to love God in a state of sin completely and thus to bring forth sorrow for sin out of love of God according to the substance of the deed. See theses 37 and 38, which discuss participation in the church's benefactions.

103. Plenary indulgences allowed one application during one's lifetime and at the approach of death, and they were sometimes declared null and void for a certain period of time with the promulgation of a new indulgence. See thesis 89.

104. This objection was already in the imperial complaints (*gravamina*) of 1511. Both Leo X's bull

90. To suppress these very pointed arguments of the laity by force alone and not to resolve them by providing reasons is to expose the church and the pope to ridicule by their enemies and to make Christians miserable.

91. Therefore, if indulgences were preached according to the spirit and intention of the pope, all of these [objections] would be easily resolved—indeed, they would not exist.[105]

92. And thus,[106] away with all those prophets who say to Christ's people, "Peace, peace," and there is no peace![107]

93. May it go well for all of those prophets who say to Christ's people, "Cross, cross," and there is no cross![108]

94. Christians must be encouraged diligently to follow Christ, their head,[109] through penalties, death, and hell,

95. and in this way they may be confident of "entering heaven through many tribulations"[110] rather than through the [false] security of peace.

1517

---

proclaiming the Peter's indulgence (31 May 1515) and the *Summary Instruction* did this very thing.

105. By applying his basic premise from the earlier theses (especially thesis 5), which limited papal authority to issuing indulgences only for ecclesiastical penalties, Luther thought to solve all of these sharp objections.

106. Latin: *itaque*, introducing theses 92–95, as a kind of conclusion or peroration. See the introduction, p. 6.

107. See Jer. 6:14, 8:11; and Ezek. 13:10, 16. Peace with God comes through the promise of absolution, not the purchase of indulgences. See also thesis 39 for this difficulty.

108. In a letter from 23 June 1516, addressed to the deposed Augustinian prior in Neustadt an der Orle, Michael Dressel (d. after 1523) (WA Br 1:27, 38–46), Luther writes: "Are you ignorant, most honorable father, that God . . . places his peace in the midst of no peace, that is, in the midst of all trials? . . . Therefore, that person whom no one disturbs does not have peace—on the contrary, this is the peace of the world. Instead, that person whom everyone and everything disturbs has peace and bears all of these things with quiet joy. You are saying with Israel, 'Peace, peace, and there is no peace'; instead say with Christ, 'Cross, cross, and there is no cross.' For as quickly as the cross ceases to be cross so quickly you would say joyfully [with the hymn], 'Blessed cross, among the trees there is none such [as you].'"

109. See, for example, Col. 1:18.

110. Acts 14:22.

2

The Letter to Albrecht

On 31 October 1517 Martin Luther wrote the following letter to the highest ecclesiastical authority in the Holy Roman Empire of the German Nation, the Archbishop of Mainz, Albrecht of Brandenburg.[1] He was the younger son of Margrave Johann Cicero (1455-1499), elector of Brandenburg.[2] Upon Johann's death in 1499, his older brother Joachim I (1484-1535) succeeded their father as elector. Together in 1506, Joachim and Albrecht founded the University of Frankfurt/Oder, which Albrecht also attended. As the scion of the powerful Hohenzollern family, he became Archbishop of Magdeburg in 1513 and administrator of the diocese of Halberstadt, both just west of the lands of the Saxon elector, Frederick the Wise.

---

1. For the facts in this introduction, see Bodo Nischan, "Albert of Brandenburg," in: *The Oxford Encyclopedia of the Reformation*, ed. Hans J. Hillerbrand, 4 vols. (New York & Oxford: Oxford University Press, 1996), 1:15-16, and the introduction to the letter by Gottfried Krodel in LW 48: 43-45.
2. The term "elector" designates the seven highest princes in the Holy Roman Empire, who were constitutionally responsible for the election of the emperor. During this time this included four secular princes (the Margrave of Brandenburg, the Duke of Saxony, the Count of the Palatinate [with his central castle in Heidelberg] and the King of Bohemia [who was also the archduke of Austria]) and three ecclesiastical princes (the archbishops of Trier, Cologne and Mainz).

The next year he was named Archbishop of Mainz, one of three ecclesiastical electors in the Empire, but he ruled from Halle, a city near Magdeburg directly under the control of the archdiocese of Mainz. For the privilege of holding more than one ecclesiastical position (normally forbidden in canon law) and of receiving such a prestigious appointment, Albrecht paid 24,000 ducats (14,000 for the position and another 10,000 for the exemption).

To finance this enormous fee, he received a loan from the powerful Fugger banking family of Augsburg, which he planned to pay off using half the proceeds from the so-called "Peter's Indulgence."[3] Albrecht entrusted Johann Tetzel with the promotion of this indulgence and ordered his court theologians to write the *Summary Instruction*, which explained the benefits of this indulgence and the limits of the preaching that accompanied its sale. Upon receiving the *Ninety-Five Theses*, Albrecht, because he and his advisors suspected heresy, turned them over both to his theology faculty in Mainz for its opinion and to Rome.

A patron of the arts and music, of architecture and humanist scholarship, Albrecht continued to function as Germany's ecclesiastical leader even after the Reformation began, but under very different circumstances. He was involved in conversations with the Saxon theologians, especially Philip Melanchthon (1497-1560), at the Diet of Augsburg in 1530.[4] During the same period, however, especially in the face of the Peasants' War of 1525,[5] he more and more actively supported Luther's opponents. When his nephew Elector Joachim II (1505-1571) introduced the Reformation into

---

3. Luther knew nothing of these arrangements when he wrote the *Ninety-Five Theses*.

4. On 25 June 1530 at this same imperial diet, the Protestant princes and cities presented their confession of faith, later called the Augsburg Confession. Drafted by Philip Melanchthon, it is the basic statement of faith by Lutherans to this day.

5. An uprising of peasants and artisans that wracked German-speaking parts of the Holy Roman Empire from 1524-1525 which was finally harshly suppressed by the ruling authorities.

Brandenburg in 1539, he abandoned Halle (in 1541) and soon thereafter both Halle and Magdeburg introduced the Reformation. He died in Mainz in 1545.

Luther's letter reflects the high Renaissance style expected in any direct appeals to such a powerful ecclesiastical and political figure. What may strike modern readers as false humility simply reflected the customs of that day. Luther as friar and obscure teacher was expected to show such deference. But Luther's deference to the person of Albrecht did not prevent him in harshly criticizing practices (namely, the sale of indulgences and especially the misleading preaching accompanying them), which he doubtless knew was going on with Albrecht's full knowledge. To give Albrecht a "way out," so to speak, Luther imagined that the *Summary Instruction* went out without Albrecht's knowledge (which was hardly the case).

In any event, the letter reflected many of the issues Luther brought up in the *Ninety-Five Theses* themselves and his deep pastoral concern. Luther appended two documents to the letter to expose the questionable theology and practice surrounding indulgences.[6] The first, the *Ninety-Five Theses*, would be distributed and published in the coming months and became the focus of Luther's case with Rome. The other was a brief essay on indulgences (in some later versions mistaken for a sermon) that raised some of the same questions but was never published.[7]

The original letter is in the royal archives [*Riksarkivet*] in Stockholm, Sweden. According to a note made on the back of the letter by a secretary to Archbishop Albrecht, the letter was opened by Albrecht's advisors in Magdeburg on 17 November 1517 and sent

---

6. At around the same time Luther seems also to have sent a letter warning about Tetzel's preaching to his ordinary bishop, Jerome of Brandenburg, with which he included a copy of the *Ninety-Five Theses*.

7. See WA Br 12: 2-10; WA 1: 65-69; WA 9: 764. Some of the arguments of this second enclosure were then taken up by Luther in the *Sermon on Indulgences and Grace* (1518), below, p. 44, n. 24.

on to the Archbishop, who was at the time in Aschaffenburg (a city belonging to the archbishopric of Mainz). On 13 December 1517 the Archbishop began a process against Luther to prevent further dissemination of his arguments (by which time he had sent the documents to the University of Mainz and Rome), instructing the advisors in Magdeburg to charge Johann Tetzel with the task of informing Luther of this. On 17 December Albrecht received a mildly negative judgment against Luther's arguments from Mainz's theological faculty. The case in Rome went on unabated.

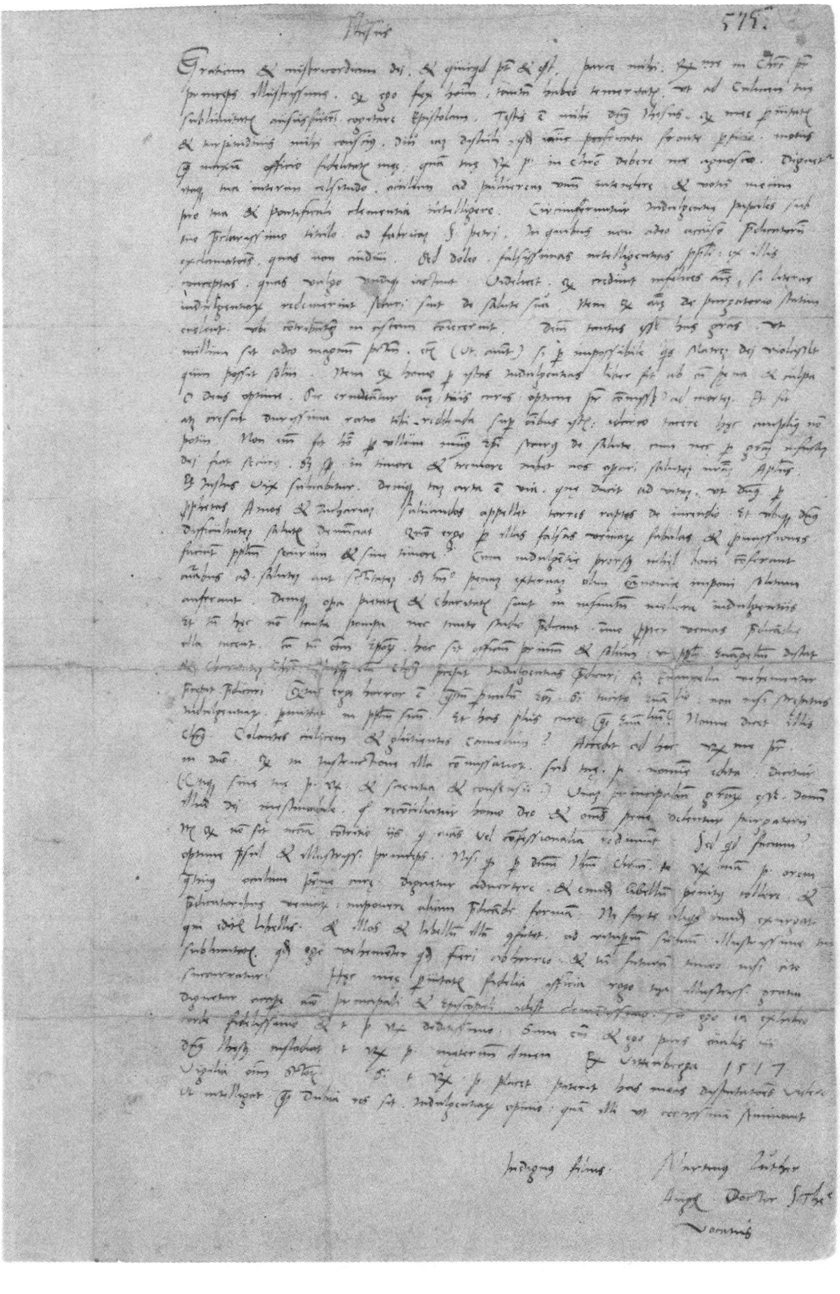

Fig. 2.1 Luther's letter to Albrecht.

Letter from Martin Luther to Albrecht, Archbishop of Mainz, Dated 31 October 1517[8]

[Martin Luther] to the Most Reverend Father in Christ, the Most Illustrious Lord, Lord Albrecht, archbishop of the churches of Magdeburg and Mainz, Primate [of German Lands], Margrave of Brandenburg, etc., to his venerably revered and most beloved lord and shepherd in Christ,

Jesus!

God's grace and mercy[9] and whatever may be and is![10] Forgive me, most Reverend Father in Christ and Most Illustrious Sovereign, that I, the dregs of humanity, have the temerity even to dare to conceive of a letter to Your Sublime Highness. The Lord Jesus is my witness, that, aware of my insignificance and unworthiness, I have up until the present put off what I am doing now "with a bold face,"[11] motivated completely by the duty of my loyalty, which I know I owe to you, Reverend Father in Christ. Therefore, may Your Highness deign in the meantime to turn your eye toward this grain of dust and, for the sake of your episcopal clemency, look into my request.

Under your most distinguished [name and] title, papal indulgences are being disseminated among the people for the construction of St. Peter's [in Rome]. In these matters, I do not so much find fault with the cries of the preachers, which I have not heard,[12] but I do

---

8. This is a revision of LW 48:43–49, a translation by Gottfried Krodel, based upon WA Br 1:108–15.

9. See 1 Tim. 1:2 and 2 Tim. 1:2, Paul's greetings to his associate. Here Luther combines his early epistolary greetings ("Jesus!"), perhaps taken from monastic practice, with a Pauline style that by 1522 he will exclusively employ in all of his letters.

10. This unusual greeting (instead of "my complete devotion" or some other demonstration of humility) occurs only one other time in Luther's correspondence, as a greeting to Frederick the Wise, elector of Saxony (WA Br 1:236, 1–5): "To the most illustrious . . . Frederick, Elector . . . . Brother Martin Luther Augustinian [wishes] felicity and whatever else the prayer of a sinner can." For a discussion of the style of this letter, see the introduction, p. 29.

11. Erasmus, *Adages*, I, 8, 47, citing Seneca and others; or it could be translated "shamelessly."

12. Due to the fact that Elector Frederick of Saxony had forbade the selling of this indulgence in

bewail the people's completely false understanding, gleaned from these fellows, which they spread everywhere among the common folk. For example, these poor souls believe: that if they were to purchase these letters of indulgence they would then be assured of their salvation;[13] likewise, that souls immediately leap from purgatory when they have thrown a contribution into the chest;[14] and then that the graces [of indulgences] are so great that no sin is of such magnitude that it cannot be forgiven—even if (as they say) someone should rape the Mother of God, were this possible;[15] likewise, that through these indulgences a person is freed from every penalty and guilt.[16]

O great God! In this way, excellent Father, souls committed to your care are being directed to death. A most severe reckoning has fallen on you above all others and is indeed growing.[17] For that reason I could no longer keep silent about these things. For a human being does not attain security about salvation through any episcopal function, since a person does not even become secure through the infused grace of God.[18] But instead the Apostle [Paul] orders us constantly to "work out our salvation in fear and trembling."[19] "It is [even] hard for the righteous to be saved."[20] Furthermore, "the way is [so] narrow that leads to life,"[21] that the Lord through the

his territories, fearing a drain of gold and less appeal for the indulgences received by viewing the relics housed in the Castle Church in Wittenberg.

13. See thesis 32, p. 18.
14. See thesis 27, p. 17.
15. See thesis 75, p. 23, an exaggeration Tetzel denied having made. Christians in the sixteenth century held to the perpetual virginity of Mary.
16. See theses 21 and 76, pp. 16 and 23, respectively.
17. See thesis 80, p. 24.
18. A technical term for the grace received through the sacrament of penance. See the introduction, pp. xv-xvii. Medieval theology and practice, relying on Augustine's (354–430) definition of pride as the chief sin, insisted that security regarding salvation was a sign of pride. Luther, by contrast, would come to argue that assurance of forgiveness rested in God's word. See thesis 7, p. 14, n. 33.
19. Phil. 2:12.
20. 1 Pet. 4:18.

prophets Amos and Zechariah calls those who will be saved "a brand plucked from the fire."[22] The Lord, too, announces the difficulty of salvation everywhere. How then can the [indulgence preachers] make the people secure and unafraid through those false tales and promises linked to indulgences, given that indulgences confer upon souls nothing of benefit for salvation or holiness but only remove external penalty, once customarily imposed by the [penitential] canons?[23]

Furthermore, works of godliness and love are infinitely better than indulgences, and yet [the indulgence preachers] do not preach such things with the same kind of pomp and effort.[24] On the contrary, they remain silent about those works for the sake of preaching indulgences, even though it is the first and sole office of all bishops that the people learn the gospel and the love of Christ. For Christ nowhere commanded indulgences to be preached, but he strongly commanded the gospel to be preached.[25] Therefore, what a horror, what a danger to a bishop if—while the gospel is being silenced—he only permits the clamoring of indulgences among his people and is more concerned with them than the gospel! Did not Christ say to them, "You strain out a gnat but swallow a camel"?[26]

Added to this, my Reverend Father in the Lord, is the fact that in that [Summary] Instruction for the indulgence commissioners,[27] published under Your Fatherly name, it is stated (surely without the consent or knowledge of your Reverend Father) that one of the principal graces [of this Peter's indulgence] is that inestimable gift of God by which a human being is reconciled to God and

---

21. Matt. 7:14 (following a literal translation of the Greek and the Latin).
22. Amos 4:11 and Zech. 3:2.
23. See thesis 5, p. 14, the heart of Luther's argument in the *Ninety-Five Theses*, and thesis 8, p. 14f).
24. See theses 41 and 55, pp. 19 and 21, respectively.
25. Mark 16:15. See theses 53–54, p. 21.
26. Matt. 23:24.
27. For more on this booklet, see the introduction, p. 2.

all the penalties of purgatory are blotted out.[28] Likewise, [it stated] that contrition is not necessary for those who purchase souls [from purgatory][29] or acquire confessional privileges.[30]

But what can I do, Most Excellent Prelate and Most Illustrious Sovereign, except beseech you, Most Reverend Father, through our Lord Jesus Christ that you may deign to turn your fatherly eye toward [this matter] and completely withdraw this little book and impose upon the preachers of indulgences another form of preaching? Otherwise, perhaps someone may arise who by publishing pamphlets may refute those [preachers] and that booklet [the *Summary Instruction*]—to the greatest disgrace of Your Most Illustrious Highness—something that I indeed would strongly hate to have happen, and yet I fear that it may happen in the future unless things are quickly remedied.[31]

I beg Your Most Illustrious Grace to deign to accept in a princely and episcopal, that is, in the kindest way this faithful service of my humble self, just as I, too, with a most faithful and devoted heart am presenting these things to you, Reverend Father. For I, too, am a part

28. See theses 11 and 32, pp. 15 and 18, respectively. The *Summary Instruction* states: "The first grace [of this indulgence] is the complete remission of all sins; and nothing greater than this can be named, since the sinner, deprived of God's grace, obtains complete remission by these means and once more enjoys God's grace; moreover through this remission of sins the punishment that one is obliged to suffer in purgatory on account of the affront to the Divine Majesty is all remitted and the pains of purgatory completely blotted out." This revised translation is from Henry Bettenson and Chris Maunder, eds., *Documents of the Christian Church*, 4th ed. (Oxford: Oxford University Press, 2011), 195.

29. See thesis 35, p. 18. The *Summary Instruction* (Bettenson and Maunder, *Documents*, 196f.) states: "The fourth important grace is for those souls in purgatory, and it is the complete remission of all sins . . . It is furthermore not necessary that the persons who place their contributions in the chest for the dead should be contrite in heart and have orally confessed . . ."

30. See thesis 35, p. 18, n. 16. The *Summary Instruction* (Bettenson and Maunder, *Documents*, 196) states: "The second principal grace is a 'confessional' [confessional letter] replete with the greatest, most important, and hitherto unheard of privileges . . ." These included choosing one's own confessor and forgiving sins usually reserved to the pope.

31. See theses 81–90, pp. 24–26. Whether Luther had himself in mind here is uncertain. However, the publication of the *Ninety-Five Theses* and the German *Sermon on Indulgences and Grace* certainly caused this very thing.

of your flock. May the Lord Jesus protect you forever, Most Reverend Father! Amen.

From Wittenberg, 1517, on the Eve of All Saints' Day.[32]

If it pleases the Reverend Father, he could examine my disputation [theses],[33] so that he may understand how dubious a thing this opinion about indulgences is, an opinion that those [preachers] disseminate with such complete certainty.

Your unworthy son,
Martin Luther
Augustinian, called as Doctor of Sacred Theology[34]

---

32. 31 October.
33. The *Ninety-Five Theses*. See above, pp. 13–26.
34. Luther justified his attacks on indulgences in part on the basis of his responsibility as an officially called Doctor of Sacred Theology. The oath of loyalty to the church and its Scriptures that he took upon receiving his doctorate, he later argued, compelled him to speak out.

3

─────

A Sermon on Indulgences and Grace

In the months after the distribution and publication of the *Ninety-Five Theses*, reactions came from both friend and foe. Suspecting they contained heresy, the archbishop of Mainz, Albrecht von Brandenburg, sent copies to his theological faculty for their judgment (they responded on 13 December 1517) and to Rome for its opinion. By August 1518 the papal court's theologian, Sylvester Prierias, published a lengthy refutation. But much earlier, on 20 January 1518 at the University of Frankfurt/Oder (only a little over 100 miles east of Wittenberg), a University founded by Albrecht and his brother, Johann Tetzel himself defended 106 theses refuting Luther's position, composed with the help of Conrad Wimpina, a professor of theology there. The occasion was also a regular meeting of the leaders of the Saxon Dominican friaries. By March a printed version of these theses had fallen into Luther's hands.[1]

─────

1. For details, see *Die 106 Frankfurter Thesen*, in: *Dokumente zur Causa Lutheri (1517-1521)*, pt. 1: *Das Gutachten des Prierias und weitere Schriften gegen Luthers Ablaßthesen (1517-1518)*, ed. Peter Fabisch and Erwin Iserloh (Münster: Aschendorff, 1988), 310-20.

At the same time, Luther had also learned about the publication of the *Ninety-Five Theses* in Nuremberg through his contact there, Christopher Scheurl. We know from Scheurl's correspondence with others earlier in January 1518 that he and others in Nuremberg intended to translate them into German; something that another Nuremberger, Caspar Nützel (1471-1529), proceeded to do. By March Luther had received copies of the Latin and German versions and wrote back on 5 March 1518, not simply thanking Scheurl for copies but also complaining that a bare translation of the *Ninety-Five Theses* into German was "not fitting for educating the common folk."[2] Indeed, it is not at all clear (given that *no* printed copies of a German translation of the *Ninety-Five Theses* from this period exist) whether Scheurl sent Luther a *printed* translation or, as seems more likely, simply a manuscript of Nützel's translation. In any case, Luther made it clear that he wanted to provide something more fitting for the German reader. The result was the *Sermon on Indulgences and Grace.*[3]

The *Sermon* used more basic language and categories to talk about the nature of the Sacrament of Penance and indulgences than had the *Ninety-Five Theses*, it summarized points contained there, and because it was written at the same time as Luther was working on the *Explanations of the Ninety-Five Theses* it reflected the language and arguments found in that document. But at several points it also responded directly to Tetzel's theses.[4] Its popularity far surpassed that of the *Ninety-Five Theses*, with at least twenty-four printings between 1518 and 1520. Indeed, this tract more than any other catapulted Luther into the public eye and made him a best-selling author overnight. Here Luther's clear explanations of complicated

---

2. WA Br 1:152, 12-13.
3. This reconstruction disagrees slightly with WA 1: 239. See Brecht, 208 for corrections.
4. For specifics, see below.

theological arguments and his edgy style, in which he repeatedly attacked scholastic theologians and their "opinions," made a splash with the German reading public. Whatever may have been generally known about the dispute before March 1518, the publication of this *Sermon* transformed Luther into a new, popular writer throughout Germany, one who very likely was saying publicly what at least some of his contemporaries may well have been thinking and sharing privately: that the bases for certain aspects of the sale of indulgences were theologically shaky. Moreover, his criticisms of scholastic theology had much in common with similar attacks by other popular humanists and would have endeared him to his Renaissance-minded readers. Lacking from this sermon, however, was any reference to papal authority, a sure indication that Luther's real target was not the pope, who (he thought) would agree with his arguments, but scholastic theologians and canon (ecclesiastical) lawyers.

With Luther having now crossed over into the vernacular, Tetzel also felt constrained to respond in German, publishing in April his *Refutation Made by Brother Johann Tetzel, Dominican and Inquisitor of Heretics against an Impudent Sermon of Twenty Erring Articles concerning the Papal Indulgence and Grace: For All Christian Believers to Know and Note.*[5] He labored to show just how heretical Luther's statements were and warned Christians not to be seduced by what Luther wrote. In contrast to Luther's bestseller, no one reprinted Tetzel's work. Luther responded to Tetzel's refutation in *The Freedom of the "Sermon on Papal Indulgences and Grace" of Doctor Martin Luther against the "Refutation," Being Completely Fabricated to Insult That Very Sermon* (WA 1: 380-93). Also a best seller, this defense was printed eleven times between 1518 and 1520.

---

5. For an English version, see *Johann Tetzel's Rebuttal against Luther's Sermon on Indulgences and Grace*, trans. Dewey Weiss Kramer (Atlanta: Pitts Theology Library, 2012).

Fig. 3.1 Image of Indulgence.

A Sermon on Indulgences and Grace[6]

First, you should know that some new teachers, such as the Master of Sentences, St. Thomas [Aquinas], and their disciples,[7] divide [the Sacrament of] Penance[8] into three parts: contrition, confession, and satisfaction.[9] And, although this distinction and opinion of theirs is scarcely or not at all to be found based in Holy Scripture or in the ancient holy Christian teachers,[10] nevertheless we will pass over this for now and speak using their categories.

Second, they say that indulgences do not involve the first or the second part, that is, contrition or confession, but rather satisfaction.

Third, satisfaction is further divided into three parts, that is, prayer, fasting, and almsgiving.[11] Thus, prayer includes all kinds of works proper to the soul, such as reading, meditating, hearing God's word, preaching, teaching, and the like. Fasting includes all kinds of work that mortify the flesh, such as vigils, working,[12] [sleeping on a] hard

---

6. The following translation of *Ein Sermon von Ablaß und Gnade* is based upon WA 1:239–46.

7. Peter Lombard (c. 1096–1160), and Thomas Aquinas (c. 1225–1274), a Dominican Scholastic theologian. At this time, Luther understood his struggle to be against Dominicans who overwhelmingly favored papal authority.

8. Buß or *poenitentia* has three meanings in English: the sacrament of penance, penitence, and repentance.

9. See Peter Lombard, *Sentences*, IV d. 16, q. 1, and all medieval teachers after him: "In the perfection of penance three things must be observed, namely compunction of the heart, confession of the mouth and satisfaction of works." Lombard claimed to derive this from John Chrysostom, *De poenitentia*, dist. 1, chap. "Perfecta." Lombard's medieval commentators defined contrition as sorrow for sin out of love of God (as opposed to attrition, which was sorrow for sin out of fear of punishment) and confession as the recitation of all of one's mortal sins to a priest. Depending on the medieval school of thought, at the moment of either contrition or confession a person had the guilt of his or her sins forgiven, was moved from a state of sin to a state of grace, and had his or her punishment reduced from eternal punishment (hell) to temporal punishment. Satisfaction, imposed by the confessor, was thus a matter of satisfying the remaining temporal punishment by doing good works.

10. Alongside Scripture, Luther maintained throughout his career that ancient church teachers also had authority, albeit under God's Word. See also Luther's point 20 below, p. 47f.

11. See the Sermon on the Mount in Matt. 6:1–18, from which these categories arose.

12. The monastic vow of the Benedictines was often summarized as *ora et labora* (prayer and work).

bed, [wearing rough] clothes, etc. Almsgiving includes all kinds of good works of the body and mercy toward the neighbor.

Fourth, all of these [teachers] hold for a certainty that indulgences take away these very works of satisfaction that ought to be done for sin or are required[13] to be done. For an indulgence is supposed to take away all these works so that nothing good remains for us to do.

Fifth, among many [teachers] it is an open and unresolved debate whether indulgences also take away even more than such good works as are required, namely whether they also remove the punishment for sin that God's righteousness demands.[14]

Sixth, for the moment I will put their opinions aside without refuting them.[15] This is what I say: No one can defend the position with any passage from Scripture that God's righteousness desires or demands any punishment or satisfaction from sinners except for their heartfelt and true contrition or conversion alone—with the condition that from that moment on they bear the cross of Christ[16] and practice the aforementioned works (but not as imposed by anyone). For this is what God said through Ezekiel [18:21 with 33:14–16, paraphrase]: "If the wicked turn away from all their sins . . . and do . . . right, so will I no longer think on their sins."[17] Thus, in the same way he himself absolved Mary Magdalene [Luke 7:36–50],[18] the paralytic [Mark 2:1–12], the woman taken in adultery [John 8:1–11], etc.[19] I

13. The confessor or canon (church) law determined certain temporal penalties for each mortal sin as part of the sacrament of penance. See above, pp. xvi–xix.
14. Here Luther may be referring to differences among such teachers as Thomas Aquinas, Bonaventure (c. 1221–1274) and Gabriel Biel (c. 1420–1495), where the latter two argued that normal works of satisfaction were better than indulgences.
15. At this point in the dispute, Luther does not see himself attacking church doctrine but, rather, the "opinions" of Scholastic theologians, opinions that he views as unfounded in Scripture or tradition. From this point on, his arguments reflect the *Ninety-Five Theses*, here theses 1–4 and 39–40.
16. See Matt. 16:24.
17. Luther again used this passage in his *Explanations of the Ninety-Five Theses*, on thesis 5 (LW 31:96).
18. The traditional medieval understanding of these texts was that Mary Magdalene anointed Jesus.

would like to hear who would prove the opposite—besides the fact that some doctors have made this up.

Seventh, in point of fact one finds that God punishes some according to his righteousness or through punishment impels them to contrition as in Psalm 89 [:30–33]: "If his [David's] children forsake my law . . . then I will punish their transgressions with the rod . . . but I will not remove my steadfast love from them."[20] But this punishment is in no one's power to lessen, except God's alone. Indeed, God will not relax such punishment but instead promises to impose it.

Eighth, for this reason, because no one has a name for this made-up punishment [of Scholastic teachers] and does not know what it is, therefore if this penalty is nothing, then the above-mentioned good work [of procuring indulgences] is nothing.

Ninth, I say that even if this very day the Christian church decided and decreed that indulgences took away more than the works of satisfaction did,[21] nevertheless it would still be a thousand times better that no Christian buy or desire indulgences but instead that they would rather do works and suffer punishment. For indulgences are and may continue to be nothing other than the neglect of good works and salutary suffering, which a person should rather choose than omit—even though some of the new preachers have invented two kinds of sufferings: *Medicativae, Satisfactoriae*,[22] that is, some

19. Luther employed these and other examples in his *Explanations of the Ninety-Five Theses*, to thesis 7 (LW 31:101f.).

20. Luther also referred to this text in his *Explanations* to thesis 5 (LW 31:89–97) and in his *Asterisks* against Johann Eck (WA 1:285, 2f.), which were both being composed in the spring of 1518.

21. See statement 5 above, p. 42.

22. This is the only place in this tract where Luther employs Latin terms meaning "for medication" or "for satisfaction." He is citing terms employed by Johann Tetzel and Konrad Wimpina ("new preachers," as Luther labels them here) in their attack on the *Ninety-Five Theses*: *Die 106 Frankfurter Thesen*, in: *Dokumente zur Causa Lutheri*, 323 and 331 (theses 14 and 72). Thomas Aquinas uses a similar distinction in *Quodlibet* II, q. 8, a. 2, ad 3, but to a different end: "It must be said that satisfaction is both punitive (insofar as it is an act of vindictive justice) and also medicative (insofar as it is something sacramental). Thus, indulgences complete the role

suffering is for satisfaction and some for improvement. But, praise God, we have more freedom to disdain this kind of prattle than they have freedom to dream it up. For all suffering, indeed, everything God lays upon Christians is for their betterment and benefit.

Tenth, nothing is being said [by arguing] that the punishment and works may be too much, that the individual may not complete them because of the shortness of life, and therefore there is need for indulgences for such a person.[23] I respond that this has no basis in fact and is pure fiction. For God and the holy church impose on no one more than they are able to carry, as St. Paul also says [1 Cor. 10:13, paraphrase]: "God will not let [anyone] be tested beyond [what that person can endure]." And this heaps no small insult upon Christianity when someone accuses it of imposing heavier burdens than we can bear.

Eleventh, although the satisfaction set in canon law is still on the books—that for each mortal sin seven years of satisfaction is imposed—nevertheless Christianity must let these very laws go and impose nothing more than what they allow each to bear. Much more, given that this [rule] is not in force, should one take care not to impose more than any one person will be able to bear.[24]

Twelfth, it is fine to say that the sinner with residual punishment

---

of satisfaction insofar as it is punitive because indeed the punishment, which someone else underwent, is imputed to another person as if that one had undergone it, and therefore it takes away the actual punishment. But it does not take the place of satisfaction insofar as it is medicative, because there remain the inclinations toward sinning that are left behind from the previous sin, for the cleansing of which there is necessarily the work of satisfaction."

23. This is another direct attack on Tetzel and Wimpina's *Die 106 Frankfurter Thesen*, in *Dokumente zur Causa Lutheri*, 336.

24. Canon law, a medieval compilation of papal and conciliar decrees and statements of the church fathers first made by Gratian (twelfth century), reflected in its section on penance the earlier practice of public punishment for members of the church who committed serious crimes and could only be reconciled to the church after seven years of penitence. These punishments were then applied to all mortal sins (serious misdeeds, the immorality of which the perpetrator understands and to which her or she consents). Luther already makes this objection in the *Tractatus de Indulgentiis* (WA 1:65–69, here 65, 25–31; and WA Br 12:2–10, here lines 19–25), which he appended to his letter to Albrecht.

should be directed to purgatory or to indulgences. But more must be said about the basis and underpinnings for this.

Thirteenth, it is a tremendous error when people imagine that they can make satisfaction for their sins, which God instead always forgives gratis out of immeasurable grace while desiring nothing for this [grace] except that one live well from then on.[25] Whenever Christianity demands something further, it may and should set such a thing aside and not impose anything heavy or unbearable.

Fourteenth, indulgences are tolerated for the sake of the imperfect and lazy Christians, who either do not want to practice good works in a lively way or want to avoid suffering. For indulgences do not demand improvement but tolerate and accept such people as imperfect. For this reason, one should not speak against indulgences, but one must also not speak in favor of using them.

Fifteenth, a person who gives to build St. Peter's [in Rome], or whatever else is mentioned [in indulgence preaching], purely for God's sake is acting in a far better and more certain way than those who take an indulgence for it. For it is dangerous when they give such a gift for the sake of an indulgence and not for God's sake.

Sixteenth, a work shown to the poor is much better than one given toward [constructing] a building, and it is also much better than when an indulgence is given for such a work.[26] For, as stated above, a good deed done is much better than many avoided. Indulgences, however, mean avoiding many good works, or else nothing is avoided.

Furthermore, so that I may instruct you correctly,[27] please note the following. If you want to give something, you ought above all else (without considering St. Peter's building or indulgences) give to

---

25. This point (that forgiveness arises from God's grace alone) and the next, also made in the *Ninety-Five Theses*, no. 36, will become increasingly important for Luther.
26. See the *Ninety-Five Theses*, nos. 42–46.
27. This is one place where a more homiletical style occurs, pointing to this piece's sermonic origin.

your poor neighbor. When it comes to the point that there is no one in your city who needs help (unless God deigns it, this will never happen!), then you ought to give where you want: to churches, altars, decorations, or chalices that are for your own city. And when that, too, is no longer necessary, then first off—if you wish—you may give to the building of St. Peter's or anywhere else. Moreover, you should not do this for the sake of an indulgence, for St. Paul says [1 Tim. 5:8], "And whoever does not provide for . . . family members, is no Christian and is worse than an unbeliever."[28] And avoid those who tell you differently, who deceive you or who search for your soul in a moneybag. And when they find a penny in the purse, it is dearer to them than any soul whatsoever.[29]

Suppose you say, "Then I will never again buy an indulgence." I respond, "That is what I already said above. My will, desire, plea, and counsel are that no one buy an indulgence. Let the lazy and sleepy Christians buy indulgences. You run from them."

Seventeenth, indulgences are neither commanded nor recommended. Instead they count among the things that are permitted and allowed. Therefore, it is not a work of obedience and also not meritorious but instead a departure from obedience. Therefore, although one should not hinder someone from buying them, nevertheless one should draw Christians away from them and arouse and encourage them to do those works and [suffer those] punishments that indulgences avoid.[30]

Eighteenth, whether souls are rescued from purgatory through indulgences, I do not know and I also do not believe it, although

28. The NRSV has "has denied the faith." Luther also used this text in his *Explanations of the Ninety-Five Theses* to thesis 47 (LW 31:204).
29. The greed of indulgence preachers, a common trope at the time, is also reflected in the *Ninety-Five Theses*.
30. Here, as in the *Ninety-Five Theses*, Luther is instructing preachers. By insisting that he is not hindering purchase of indulgences, Luther was attempting to stay within the strictures of canon law and the decrees surrounding the "Peter's Indulgence."

some new doctors [of the church] say it.[31] But it is impossible for them to prove it, and the church has not yet decided the matter.[32] Therefore, for the sake of greater certainty, it is much better that each of you prays and works for these souls. For this has more value and is certain.

Nineteenth, in these points I have no doubt, and they are sufficiently grounded in the Scripture. Therefore, all of you should have no doubts about it and let the scholastic doctors alone. Taken altogether, they do not have enough with their opinions to put together a single sermon.

Twentieth, although some (for whom such truth really damages their treasure chests)[33] now want to call me a heretic, nevertheless I consider such blathering no big deal,[34] especially since the only ones doing this are some darkened minds, who have never even smelled a Bible, who have never read a Christian teacher, and who do not even understand their own teachers but instead remain stuck with their shaky and close-minded opinions. For if they had understood them, they would have known that they should not defame anyone without

---

31. Purgatory (a place of purgation) was understood to be an interim state between death and the beatific vision (heaven), designed to purge a soul of any remaining impurities and thereby satisfying the remaining punishment for mortal sins. Although the suffering in purgatory was understood to be worse than any on earth, the souls could only leave purgatory for heaven. Souls that died in a state of sin went directly to hell. Luther here is referring to a relatively new doctrine that applied indulgences to souls in purgatory, first decreed by Pope Sixtus IV (1414–1484) in his 1476 papal bull.

32. Luther invokes the standard defense of the teacher's freedom to debate matters not yet decided by a church council. At the Leipzig Debates in the summer of 1519, he would be forced to admit that councils, too, can err. His position here is similar to that of Bonaventure (c. 1221–1274), who argued in his *Commentary on the Sentences of Peter Lombard* that the pope had authority over purgatory only *per modum suffragii* (in the mode of one begging [God] for another). This will become one of the points debated between Luther and Cardinal Cajetan (1469–1534) in the interview in Augsburg in October 1518.

33. Luther was thinking specifically of Johann Tetzel and Konrad Wimpina, the first to attack the *Ninety-Five Theses* in print.

34. At the time the *Sermon* was published, Luther had not yet received the equally strong reactions from others, including Johann Eck (1486–1543) and Silvester Prierias.

a hearing and without refuting them. Still, may God give them and us a right understanding! Amen.

Study Guide

The writings of Martin Luther in this volume arose in a specific historical context. They speak to and within a moment of history that was a time of great change. How do we evaluate Luther's words within the original context and determine the impact of his words for future contexts, including the present day? Luther was a teacher of Bible by vocation, and these early writings were intended to raise questions and encourage conversation. In this spirit, questions are provided here for individual reflection and group discussion.

Introduction [pp. xiii-xvi]

1. Describe your understanding of how the Reformation began? What have you have seen or heard about this? How does this compare to what is presented in the Introduction?

2. What *is* an indulgence, and how does it relate to the medieval sacrament of penance?

3. Relate the parts of penance to purgatory and indulgences.

4. In Luther's earliest sermons that mentioned indulgences from 1517, what was the nature of his critique? What difference does it make to learn that Luther himself "preached" an indulgence?

5. In light of the above, what difference does it make to you

that scholars debate whether the *Ninety-Five Theses* were posted or printed?

6. What might it mean that Luther was the first living bestselling author in the world on the basis of a German sermon?

7. Luther's theology distinguished *law* and *gospel*. How do you understand these terms as he used them.

8. What in this Introduction surprised you the most? Why?

The *Ninety-Five Theses* [pp. 1-26]

1. What are ways in today's church that people try to avoid God's judgment and therefore undermine God's gracious forgiveness?

2. Identify those theses that are hardest to understand. Why is this so?

3. Thesis 5 on the limits of indulgences to ecclesiastical penalties was used by Luther's opponents as a sign of his disrespect for the papacy. How else might this thesis be understood? Why was it so important for Luther's argument?

4. A handful of theses emphasize God's grace and the gospel. How might the human propensity either to "earn" salvation or to buy a way around God's judgment undercut the gospel today?

5. How does recognizing the rhetorical structure of the theses help in understanding Luther's intent? What seemed to you the strongest arguments? The weakest?

6. In the *Ninety-Five Theses* Luther attacks attempts to manipulate God through the purchase of "indulgences." Discuss whether and where this same confusion between grace and works exists in today's church.

The Letter to Albrecht [pp. 27-36]

1. What were Luther's main pastoral concerns?

2. Given the concerns identified in the previous question, in what ways do church leaders face similar issues today? What causes people to overlook them?

3. Are there occasions today when people use such outward humility in their speech or actions? What would be the advantages or disadvantages? Why do we now generally associate this with *false* humility?

4. Archbishop Albrecht immediately suspected heresy. Why might this be a typical reaction of someone in his position?

5. Why did Luther bother to make this protest? That is, what were his underlying motivations identifiable in the content and tone of this letter?

6. If you were concerned about a particular practice or teaching of the Christian church, how and to whom might you express that concern? By what authority would you do it?

The Sermon on Indulgences and Grace [pp. 37-48]

1. Much as later French and now English are the common language of scholars, in Luther's days all scholarly work, church business and school and university lectures were conducted in Latin. How did using a vernacular tongue (German) change the contours of debate over indulgences?

2. What arguments do the *Ninety-Five Theses* and the *Sermon on Indulgences and Grace* hold in common? How might this help define what Luther thought most important early in the debate?

3. While critical of scholastic theology and its method, Luther also used aspects of academic theology in his sermon. How do Luther's arguments respect the teaching and traditions of the church? How

does this challenge the notion that Luther's theology was completely new and a break with the past?

4. What do you think of the structure of Luther's sermon? What do you note about the structure? How is this like or unlike sermons you hear? Can you imagine a single sermon being a publishing phenomenon today? Why or why not?

5. Using what Luther says in this sermon, why did he think this issue important to share with the German-speaking public?

6. Luther never mentions the papacy. What other themes absent from this sermon are found in the *Ninety-Five Theses*? Although arguments from silence are by nature speculative, what might these omissions tell us about Luther's intent?

7. The posting or publishing of a set of theses or a sermon is not commonly the way to spur public dialog today. How are important matters of public concern and debate aired?

For Further Reading

Histories of the Reformation

Lindberg, Carter. *The European Reformations*. 2d ed. Oxford: Wiley-Blackwell, 2010.

MacCulloch, Diarmaid. *The Reformation: A History*. New York: Penguin, 2004.

The Writings of Martin Luther

The Annotated Luther. 6 vols. Edited by Hans Hillerbrand, Kirsi Stjerna and Timothy J. Wengert. Minneapolis: Fortress Press, 2015-2017.

Luther's Works. [American Edition.] Edited by Jaroslav Pelikan, Helmuth Lehmann and Christopher Brown. 55+ vols. St. Louis: Concordia & Philadelphia: Fortress Press, 1955- .

Martin Luther's Basic Theological Writings. Edited by Timothy Lull and William Russell. 3d edition. Minneapolis: Fortress Press, 2012.

Biographies of Martin Luther

Bainton, Roland. *Here I Stand: A Life of Martin Luther*. New York & Nashville: Abingdon-Cokesbury, 1950.

Brecht, Martin. *Martin Luther*. 3 vols. Translated by James Schaaf. Philadelphia and Minneapolis: Fortress Press, 1985-1993.

Hendrix, Scott. *Luther*. Nashville: Abingdon, 2009.

_____. *Martin Luther: A Very Short Introduction*. Oxford: Oxford University Press, 2010.

Kittelson, James M. *Luther the Reformer: The Story of the Man and His Career*. 3rd ed. revised by Hans Wiersma. Minneapolis: Fortress Press, forthcoming.

Lull, Timothy F. and Nelson, Derek R. *Resilient Reformer: The Life and Thought of Martin Luther*. Minneapolis: Fortress Press, 2015.

Oberman, Heiko A. *Luther: Man between God and the Devil*. Translated by Eileen Walliser-Schwarzbart. New Haven: Yale University Press, 1989.

The Theology of Martin Luther

Althaus, Paul. *The Theology of Martin Luther*. Translated by Robert C. Schultz. Philadelphia: Fortress Press, 1966.

Althaus, Paul. *The Ethics of Martin Luther*. Translated by Robert C. Schultz. Philadelphia: Fortress Press, 1972.

Ebeling, Gerhard. *Luther: An Introduction to His Thought*. Translated by R. A. Wilson. Philadelphia: Fortress Press, 1970.

Forde, Gerhard. *Where God Meets Man: Luther's Down-To-Earth Approach to the Gospel*. Minneapolis: Augsburg, 1972.

Kolb, Robert. *Martin Luther: Confessor of the Faith*. Oxford: Oxford University Press, 2009.

Kolb, Robert and Charles Arand. *The Genius of Luther's Theology: A Wittenberg Way of Thinking for the Contemporary Church*. Grand Rapids: Baker, 2008.

Lohse, Bernhard. *Martin Luther's Theology: Its Historical and Systematic Development*. Translated by Roy A. Harrisville. Minneapolis: Fortress Press, 1999.

Schwarz, Hans. *True Faith in God: An Introduction to Luther's Life and Thought*, Revised and Expanded Edition, Minneapolis: Fortress Press, 2015.

Wengert, Timothy J., ed. *Harvesting Martin Luther's Reflections on Theology, Ethics, and the Church*. Grand Rapids: Eerdmans, 2004.

_____. ed. *The Pastoral Luther: Essays on Martin Luther's Practical Theology*. Grand Rapids: Eerdmans, 2009.

_____. *Reading the Bible with Martin Luther*. Grand Rapids: Baker, 2013.